HOW TO RECRUIT AND TRAIN VOLUNTEER YOUTH WORKERS

Zondervan/Youth Specialties Books

HOW TO
RECRUIT AND
TRAIN
VOLUNTEER
YOUTH
WORKERS

REACHING MORE KIDS
WITH LESS STRESS

Les Christie

ZondervanPublishingHouse

Grand Rapids, Michigan

A Division of HarperCollins*Publishers*

How to Recruit and Train Volunteer Youth Workers
Copyright © 1987, 1992 by Youth Specialties, Inc.
All rights reserved

Youth Specialties Books, 1224 Greenfield Drive,
El Cajon, California 92021, are published by
Zondervan Publishing House, Grand Rapids, Michigan 49530

Library of Congress Cataloging-in-Publication Data

Christie, Les John.
   How to recruit and train volunteer youth workers / by
Les Christie.
     p.   cm.
   Rev. ed. of: Unsung heroes. c1987.
   ISBN 0-310-35151-0
   1. Church work with youth. 2. Voluntarism—Religious
aspects—Christianity. I. Christie, Les John. Unsung heroes.
II. Title.
BV4447.C479   1992
259'.2–dc20   91–31615
                                                 CIP

Edited by Dave Lambert
Interior designed by Ann Cherryman
Cover designed by Michael Kern

Printed in the United States of America

   92   93   94   95 / CH / 10 9 8 7 6 5

This book is dedicated to the unsung heroes I have had the privilege of working with over the past 20 years—men and women who freely gave of their time, energy, money, attention, and love to bring young people to maturity in Christ:

Aafja, Al, Alice, Allan, Amy, Andy, Arlene, Arty, Barb, Barbara, Becky, Ben, Bernie, Beth, Betty, Beverly, Bill, Billy, Blake, Bob, Bobbi, Brad, Brenda, Brent, Brian, Bruce, Bryon, Bud, Cara, Carl, Carol, Caroline, Carrie, Cathy, Cecil, Charlene, Cheri, Cherie, Cheryl, Christa, Chuck, Cindy, Clyde, Connie, Craig, Dan, Danny, Darlene, Dave, David, Debbie, Debby, Denise, Derek, Diana, Diane, Dick, Dinah, Dixie, Don, Donna, Doug, Duane, Dwight, Earl, Ed, Edna, Elizabeth, Elmer, Forrest, Fran, Frank, Fred, Gary, Gene, George, Gina, Ginny, Gladys, Glenn, Greg, Gretchen, Hank, Hazel, Heather, Heidi, Helen, Howard, Ignacio, Irene, Isabelle, Jack, Jackie, Jane, Janet, Jason, Jean, Jeff, Jennifer, Jerry, Jim, Jo, Joe, John, Joyce, Judy, Julie, June, Karen, Karla, Katherine, Kathleen, Kathy, Katy, Keith, Kelly, Ken, Kent, Kevin, Kim, Krista, Kurt, Lance, Larry, Laura, Laurie, Lester, Linda, Lisa, Lois, Lora, Lori, Lynn, Margaret, Marilyn, Mark, Marsha, Mary, Mary Ann, Mary Jane, Mary Jo, Melody, Michael, Mike, Millie, Mitch, Monroe, Monte, Murray, Nancy, Naomi, Nat, Neal, Nola, Norm, Otto, Pam, Pat, Patty, Paul, Paula, Peggy, Phil, Phyllis, Ralph, Randy, Ray, Rhea, Rhonda, Rick, Rob, Robert, Roberta, Robin, Rod, Roger, Ron, Rose Mary, Roy, Ruby, Ruth, Sam, Scott, Sharon, Sheldon, Sondra, Sterling, Steve, Steven, Sue, Susan, Tammy, Terri, Thelma, Tim, Tom, Ursula, Val, Verian, Veronica, Vickie, Vinny, Wally, Walt, Warren, Wayne, and of course, Wyman.

ABOUT THE YOUTHSOURCE™ PUBLISHING GROUP

YOUTHSOURCE™ books, tapes, videos, and other resources pool the expertise of three of the finest youth-ministry resource providers in the world:

Campus Life Books—publishers of the award-winning *Campus Life* magazine, who for nearly fifty years have helped high schoolers live Christian lives.

Youth Specialties—serving ministers to middle-school, junior-high, and high-school youth for over twenty years through books, magazines, and training events such as the National Youth Workers Convention.

Zondervan Publishing House—one of the oldest, largest, and most respected evangelical Christian publishers in the world.

Campus Life	Youth Specialties	Zondervan
465 Gundersen Dr.	1224 Greenfield Dr.	Grand Rapids, MI 49506
Carol Stream, IL 60188	El Cajon, CA 92021	616/698-6900
708/260-6200	619/440-2333	

Contents

Introduction

> We do many things on a volunteer basis because we want that feeling, which our nine-to-five jobs may not be giving us, of using our skills, making a difference, and being appreciated. So the assembly-line worker coaches a Little League team and knows the satisfaction of teaching, advising, and making decisions. The secretary sings in the church choir or staffs a crisis-center hotline, where she gains the feeling of being depended on and having people look up to her.[1]

When I started in youth work twenty years ago, I did it all. I tried to be everything to every kid in the youth group. I was the Lone Ranger—and I was exhausted. I was overcommitted, overworked, overwhelmed, and over a barrel.

After a few years, I was looking for the bench. I needed help fast. I had too many guilt feelings that I don't think God intended for me to have. And when I found myself inadequate and couldn't meet a particular need or didn't see immediate success, I'd walk home with a sense of depression and failure, saying, "You know, if you were just a little more adequate you'd know how to deal with that."

By the time I had reached my second youth ministry position, I had figured out that there were some obvious advantages in having other people working beside me. I recruited people to be youth volunteers. They showed up at events, assisted where needed, and built relationships with the kids. When I wasn't able to be there, they took over. But I still had a problem—the same problem experienced by Len Kageler, a top-notch youth worker in Seattle: "Because I was intimidated by people older than me, the youth staff consisted of people my age (mid-20's) and younger. We all got along well, but there was still a large turnover of staff."[2]

Most youth workers are drawn to youth ministry by their love for young people and desire to serve. But a primary task of the youth worker is also to develop other adults who will in turn work with young people. The long-term effectiveness of youth ministry depends on the ability of the youth worker to develop a team of committed adult volunteers. Regardless of the size or condition of your church, the challenge is the same. How can we recruit Christian adults to join in changing the lives of young people within the context of the local church?[3]

I hope this book will answer some of the commonly articulated questions raised by both volunteers and paid professionals. This is a practical, hands-on, how-to book. I am hoping it is not merely theory or pie-in-the-sky theology about volunteers. I will be honest and candid in sharing the pitfalls and frustrations, as well as the joys and thrills, of working with a volunteer team.

In many churches, a faithful core of people do almost everything. Continue to rely on these faithful few, and they will eventually head for the sidelines. Churches that rely on so few resemble the quadriplegic who said, "I have all the parts—I just need to be rewired."[4] I am convinced that church pews are filled with all the parts necessary for a dynamic youth ministry. Rewire those parts, and the results will surprise everyone.

I also realize that each youth ministry has its own "fingerprint," its own uniqueness. What works in one group doesn't always work in another. How the underlying principles of this book apply in one group, therefore, isn't necessarily how they'll apply in another. But I do think that these principles are universal enough in Christian churches to have some application in *every* group, and I hope that you'll be able to adapt them to suit your own ministry setting.

Several years ago I came across a wonderful parable. An insurance policyholder had sent in a claim regarding an accident he had had on the job, and the insurance company requested more information. Here's his answer:

I am writing in response to your request concerning clarification of the information I supplied in block number eleven on the insurance form, which asked for the cause of the injury. I answered, "Trying to do the job alone." I trust the following explanation will be sufficient.

I am a bricklayer by trade. On the date of the injury, I was working alone, laying brick around the top of a three-story building. When I finished the job, I had about 500 lbs. of brick left over. Rather than carry the bricks down by hand, I decided to put them into a barrel and lower them by a pulley that was fastened to the top of the building.

I secured the end of the rope at ground level, went back up to the top of the building, loaded the bricks into the barrel, and pushed it over the side. I then went back down to the ground and untied the rope, holding it securely to insure the slow descent of the barrel. As you will note on block number six of the insurance form, I weigh 145 lbs. At the shock of being jerked off the ground so swiftly by the 500 lbs. of bricks in the barrel, I lost my presence of mind—and forgot to let go of the rope.

Between the 2nd and 3rd floors I met the barrel. This accounts for the bruises and lacerations on my upper body. Fortunately, I retained enough presence of mind to maintain my tight hold on the rope and proceeded rapidly up the side of the building, not stopping until my right hand was jammed in the pulley. This accounts for my broken thumb (see block number four). Despite the pain, I continued to hold tightly to the rope. Unfortunately, at approximately the same time the barrel hit the ground, and the bottom fell out of the barrel. Devoid of the weight of the bricks, the barrel now weighed about 50 lbs. I again refer you to block number six, where my weight is listed. I began a rapid descent.

In the vicinity of the 2nd floor I met the barrel coming up. This explains the injury to my legs and lower body. Slowed only slightly, I continued my descent, landing on the pile of bricks. Fortunately, my back was only sprained. I am sorry to report, however, that at this point I again lost my presence of mind—and let go of the rope.

I trust this answers your concern. Please note that I am finished trying to do the job alone. [5]

1.
WHY VOLUNTEERS?

LET'S THROW OUT THE ONE-MAN BANDS

I've seen them on sidewalks in San Francisco. They're always fascinating, those artists placed strategically in the midst of all those musical instruments. It's almost comical— several instruments being played simultaneously by one frantic musician, who's also belting out a familiar song. I watch for a moment or two, applaud or toss some coins in a hat or guitar case—and then pass on. If the goal is merely to entertain, they are definitely successful. But if the goal is to make beautiful music, then one-man bands leave something to be desired. To make beautiful music, how much better it is to have several people, each playing the one instrument he knows best, blended and orchestrated into one finely tuned group.

I know a lot of one-man-band youth workers. I realize that their goal is not merely to entertain—but how sadly comical they are as they frantically try to do everything themselves. No one—no volunteer and no paid staff member—can do it all in youth work.

The Lone-Ranger youth worker soon resembles the circus performer in a plate-spinning act. He starts by spinning a few plates on a couple of long, thin wooden poles. No problem. Then he adds a few more plates, a few more poles—quickly running back to give the original ones another spin—and then adds a few more poles and plates, frantic now, always on the move, trying to keep all the plates spinning simultaneously, faster and faster. Definitely entertaining. But, if his goal was merely to keep 40 plates spinning on 40 poles, think how much easier it would have been to recruit ten friends to take four plates each. True, no crowd would have watched in amazement and showered the exhausted performer with applause, but is that really our purpose in youth work?[1]

Unfortunately, for too many youth workers, that *is* their purpose. They've lost sight of their original goal and got caught up in the excitement of the crowd egging them on to do more until they finally drop from exhaustion in the middle of some youth activity. It is so easy for the applause to win out over doing effective ministry.

So—what *is* the purpose of youth ministry?

"Like arrows in the hands of a warrior are sons born in one's youth. Blessed is the man whose quiver is full of them" (Psalm 127:4–5). Though directed primarily to parents, these verses also have something to say to youth workers about the purpose of youth work. If children and youth are like arrows, they must be aimed in a specific direction. If God has given us the task of caring for some of His "arrows," we must be sure we are guiding them toward the right target.

God has not left us wondering what that target might be. Colossians 1:28 states it clearly: "We proclaim Him, admonishing and teaching everyone with all wisdom so that we may present everyone perfect [mature, complete, whole] in Christ." The apostle Paul tells us we are also "to prepare God's people for works of service [ministry]" (Ephesians 4:12). Our job as youth workers is a sobering one. We are to bring young people to maturity in Christ and help prepare them for some form of ministry. We are to develop the leadership potential in youth.

Some youth workers, although they would adamantly deny it, in reality must think they are better than Jesus. Jesus discipled twelve people. How many young people are in your youth ministry? Most educators recommend one adult to every 6 to 12 young people. One-leader youth programs become self-limiting. They are limited in the number of people they can reach and the depth of individual ministry they can provide. In order for the ministry to expand, there must be other adult workers. Delegation is a must, not only to maintain the youth worker's sanity, but to accomplish God's purpose effectively.

The following description of geese illustrates how much more can be accomplished if we work as a team:

Geese

Geese don't get high-powered press coverage like sea gulls.
They're seen as dull, ordinary birds
which only attract notice twice a year
during migration . . .

Like the Blue Angels, they fly wing tip to wing tip . . .
You can hear the beat of their wings
whistling through the air in unison . . .

And that's the secret of their strength . . .
Together, cooperating as a flock,
geese can fly a 71-percent longer range . . .
The lead goose cuts a swath
through the air resistance, which creates
a helping uplift for the two birds behind him.

In turn, their beating makes it easier on the birds
behind them, much like the drag of a race car
sucked in behind the lead car . . .

Each bird takes his turn at being the leader.
The tired ones fan out to the edges of the V
for a breather, and the rested ones surge toward
the point of the V to drive the flock onward . . .

If a goose becomes too exhausted or ill
and has to drop out of the flock,
he is never abandoned.
A stronger member of the flock will follow
the failing, weak one to his resting place
and wait until he's well enough to fly again.[2]

NO LONE RANGERS

Some things just can't be done alone. In school I was always cautioned never to swim alone or lift weights alone. To that list I add: never do youth work alone. Lone-Ranger youth workers are ineffective. Oh, sure, they become the gurus of the groups they oversee. They stay in the spotlight on center stage. They get plenty of applause. But, in reality, they accomplish little for the Lord as they tackle youth ministry by themselves. They eventually burn out and become shoe salesmen.

Even the Lone Ranger needed Tonto. Everyone needs at least three different types of people involved in his life:

—A Paul, an older person who will invest himself in the youth worker's life;

—A Timothy, someone (or even a handful of someones) into whose lives the youth worker can invest himself; and

—A Barnabas, a peer who will stay by his side no matter what, but who is also not afraid to blow the whistle on him.

In the movie *Rocky*, Sylvester Stallone says, "You got gaps, and I got gaps. Let's fill each other's gaps."[3] Effective youth ministry is built primarily on relationships—on filling each other's gaps. Developing an adult friend in ministry—a Barnabas—frees the youth worker from an unhealthy dependency on affirmation from members of the youth group. Having a partner in ministry can sharpen thinking, clean up motives, and increase effectiveness.[4]

You have, whether you realize it or not, a tremendous need to share the load with others who are committed to youth ministry, to pour your life into the lives of your fellow youth staff and develop close-knit units; to surround yourself with a staff who have a variety of strengths, interests, and abilities; to instill in them a vision and conviction for youth ministry; to challenge each other, as "iron sharpens iron." The word "synergy" carries with it the idea that, together, we are better than either one can be alone. We need synergetic youth staffs that are filling each other's gaps.

Two years ago *Leadership* published an eye-opening article by Kenneth McGuire entitled "Belaying, a Model for Ministry." It expresses concisely our task in working with volunteers:

> Ten of us, all beginners, were climbing White Gap Mountain in North Carolina. We were using ropes in a system called belaying. I served as belayer, which means I controlled the safety rope for the person climbing the mountain. My job was to take up slack as each person climbed up to me and to hold the rope if he or she should fall on the way. It was very hard work.
>
> One climber was somewhat overweight and fell several times. Each time I was able to break her fall, but it caused great pain; the belaying rope cut into my waist with the tension of her weight on it. The whole procedure became for me a parable of my ministry.
>
> I wasn't climbing the mountain, she was. I was there to support her and I was thoroughly bound to her, but it was she who had to do the climbing. Each time she reached a difficult spot I knew she would fall, and I also knew her fall would cause me pain. I was tempted at times to grab the rope and pull her over the difficult parts. It would have been a lot easier on me.
>
> But I realized—thanks to the Holy Spirit—that if I pulled her over the difficult part each time, it would really have hurt her. She would have missed learning what it means to climb the mountain. Sure, I would have been her savior—but only for this time. There are other mountains she will have to climb, and I will not always be there to pull her over the rough spots. She had to do it mainly on her own. Well, after much pain and struggle she made it to the top. When she reached me she said, "I made it—I didn't think I'd ever get here."
>
> That was a great moment for both of us; for me because I knew that she had climbed the mountain on her own. I had done a good job of belaying for her. I had encouraged her and kept her from getting hurt. That was my job. But she had climbed the mountain.[5]

VARIETY OF ADULT MODELS

Maybe your youth group is small—six to ten kids in your high school group, five to eight in junior high. Maybe you're wondering, *Why do I need other adults working beside me? I can handle these few kids on my own.* Even if I had only a handful of kids in my group, I would still recruit other adults to work with me—not because of *my* needs, but because of the kids' needs. Kids need a variety of adult models.

Any adult who will interact with kids regularly becomes a model to them. In recruiting a team of adults, look for a variety of role models: married couples, singles, young adults, older folks. Youth will respond differently to different people. Kids need to see the quiet adults, the thinkers, the huggers, the zanies, the serious, the jocks, and the nerds. They need to see the deeply religious and experienced as well as the recently committed Christian.[6]

There are two goals for your diverse ministry team. One is to model, among yourselves, many of the relationships (such as marriage, friendship, older Christian with younger Christian, and so on) in which your youth group members will eventually find themselves. The second goal is to have at least one advisor on your staff with whom each adolescent can feel some identification. Grandmothers and grandfathers make great youth workers, but you would not want an entire team of senior saints. The same is true of college students, who tend to be energetic and lively, but often lack stability, experience, and maturity. We need an intergenerational youth ministry team.

PEOPLE, NOT PROGRAMS—RELATIONAL YOUTH MINISTRY

Programs may *attract* kids—but they will not *keep* kids. The person who made the greatest impact on your life was probably someone who spent time with you. Quality time, yes—but quantity time too. It is relationships, not programs, that mold young lives. Programs merely provide the framework for ministry to take place.

Relational youth workers spend time developing relationships with young people. These youth workers spend time getting to know kids before and after youth meetings, on the church bus, at school activities, and in their homes.

Relational youth workers genuinely care about young people (Philippians 2:20). Such youth workers are willing to give themselves away to kids. Kids know that this adult loves them unconditionally, just the way they are.

Relational youth workers are sensitive to the needs of young people. Like Jesus, they hurt for people who are hurting: "When He [Jesus] saw the crowds, He had compassion on them" (Matthew 9:36). Like Paul, they have a burning desire to minister to the needs they see in people: "We loved you so much that we were delighted to share with you not only the Gospel of God but our lives as well, because you had become so dear to us" (I Thessalonians 2:8).

Relational youth workers know their youth group members well enough to know their spiritual, physical, mental, and social condition. These youth workers invite young people to go camping, shopping, and on outings with the youth worker's family. They call students on the telephone. They look through local newspapers to see if one of their young people is mentioned in a positive way. If so, they clip it and send it to the young person to say, "I'm proud of you." They send birthday cards or just dumb "anytime" cards to youth group members.

Relational youth workers care about the youth in their own unique style. Mr. and Mrs. Robert DeBolt have raised twenty children, fourteen of whom were severely handicapped. Today the DeBolts have an empty nest and are on the speaking circuit. Some of their most demanding bookings come from corporations that want to use their methods for boosting team morale. All their handicapped children, and their own six, are now self-supporting college graduates and professional people. All put themselves through school, with plenty of moral support—but no financial backing—from their parents.

How did they accomplish it? The DeBolts' first task, when a child came into their home, was to develop self-esteem. A difficult challenge when a child does not have arms or legs, or is blind and deaf. But the DeBolts maintain that unless one can create a sense of self-worth in the child, no other messages will get across.[7]

Relational youth workers want to communicate to every teen that each is important, self-worthy, and valued by God as a unique and precious person. Everything needs to be geared to that message: learning names, listening, observing and asking questions, as well as sharing conversation.

All of this takes time and availability. It can't possibly be done alone, even within a smaller youth group of a dozen young people. How many young people can you spend quality, one-on-one time with? You need a team of adults to help you—and your young people deserve one.

BIBLICAL MANDATE

Possibly the most important reason for recruiting volunteers is that it is biblical. The Bible clearly commands us to share our ministry by involving the God-given gifts, talents, and abilities of others.

Right after Moses led the Israelites out of Egypt, as they started across the desert, Moses was a prime candidate for burnout. Jethro, Moses' father-in-law, had heard about Israel's miraculous deliverance from Egypt, and as Israel approached, he brought Moses' wife and children out into the desert to meet him (Exodus 18:1–7).

The next day, Jethro watched Moses. What he saw worried him. All day long, Moses sat and refereed problems among the people of Israel. One after another they came to Moses to get advice and counsel on how to solve their personal, family, and social problems (Exodus 18:13–16). By the end of the day Moses was exhausted, and many of the Israelites were still frustrated because they had stood in line all day and still hadn't gotten to talk with Moses.

"The thing that you are doing is not good," observed Moses' father-in-law. "You will surely wear out, both yourself and these people who are with you, for the task is too heavy for you; you cannot do it alone" (Exodus 18:17–18).

Jethro's suggestion to Moses was brilliant—so brilliant that it's still being used by management specialists in today's business world.

"You shall select out of all the people," Jethro said, "able men who fear God, men of truth, those who hate dishonest gain; and you shall place these over them, as leaders of thousands, of hundreds, of fifties, and of tens" (Exodus 18:21). In other words, Jethro suggested that Moses delegate responsibility to qualified men who could help him solve the day-to-day problems the people faced in forming their new society and culture. "This plan," implied Jethro, "will enable you to survive the pressures of your leadership task, and will also make it possible to meet the needs of the children of Israel."

Fortunately, Moses took the wise counsel of his father-in-law. He shared the load with others (Exodus 18:24–27), and the plan worked. In fact, the organizational structure that emerged to solve their social problems also worked for thwarting military attacks from their enemies.

The problem Moses faced is a problem every youth worker has wrestled with at some time in his ministry. When you are overworked and exhausted because you have not delegated as you should have, irritation sets in—then exhaustion, confusion, and loss of vision. For some reason, this tendency to do it all yourself is especially strong in *Christian* work. We Christians seem to feel morally obligated to work more than we should.

What happens when a person does everything? To begin with, he loses his distinctiveness. Each of us is gifted in certain areas. Adding more tasks or responsibilities to those areas weakens our distinctiveness. Our exercise of our gifts is diluted; our priorities are shifted; we lose direction.

It is not a sign of spirituality to work fifteen hours a day, seven days a week, and never take a vacation. It is not a sign of spirituality to groan your way through life looking humble and wanting to impress everybody else with all your hard work.

21

Jesus used delegation extensively. He spent most of his time training his disciples and others to do the work that he was doing.

Paul also was constantly training the men he surrounded himself with. He admonished Timothy to train others when he wrote to him and said, "And the things you have heard me say in the presence of many witnesses entrust to reliable men who will also be qualified to teach others" (2 Timothy 2:2).

When we insist on doing everything ourselves, we also deny to those around us the opportunity to use their God-given gifts. Don't forget that, in the end, our task is to prepare God's people for works of service (Ephesians 4:12), to encourage Christians to be doers, not just hearers (James 1:22), and to motivate each of us to serve one another in love (Galatians 5:13). When we encourage volunteers to work along side us in youth ministry, we're doing more than just filling slots in an organization—we're also helping people to discover their gifts (I Corinthians 12:12–14, Romans 12:5–8). We're giving them a chance to live out what they believe.

In her excellent book *Gifts of Grace*, Mary Schramm points out, "If using our gifts and sensing fulfillment and peace is associated with our work week, we can thank God. Many people find the best use of their gifts does not coincide with how they earn their paycheck. The sense of unfulfillment, caused by that creative being inside us, needs attention, and perhaps it is after the nine-to-five routine that the unrest is quieted. It may be in our leisure hours that we engage in the kind of ministry where we feel free to express our gifts."[7] The more a volunteer is involved with the ministry of the church, the better he feels about himself, the church, and his contribution. We each have something of value to give.

The book of Acts tells the story of how a handful of ordinary people were able to do extraordinary things. J. B. Phillips, in introducing his translation of the book of Acts, says this:

> These men did not make acts of faith, they believed; did not say prayers, they really prayed. They didn't hold conferences on psychosomatic medicine, they simply healed the sick. . . . But if they were uncomplicated by modern standards we have ruefully to admit that they were open on the God-ward side in a way that is almost unknown today. Consequently it is a matter of sober history that never before have any small body of ordinary people so moved the world that their enemies could say that these men, "have turned the world upside down."[9]

The church too often resembles American spectator sports: eighty thousand people badly in need of exercise watching twenty-two people badly in need of rest play ball. The church is to be a launching pad, not a hangar.

I am reminded of a story about a teenage boy who was preparing to teach his first Sunday school class—a group of four- and five-year-olds. When his mother asked him what he was planning to teach at the first class session, he replied, "Well, the lesson plan says to show them that each person is valuable for his or her unique capabilities, and that there is value in differences as well as in conformity . . . (pause) and if that doesn't work, I guess we'll make clay bunnies."[10]

I suspect we are all tempted, when faced with that particular lesson plan, to "make clay bunnies," or clean a closet, mow a lawn, go play tennis, or do anything that will keep us from looking seriously at what that heady statement implies. For if wc really believe that we, as persons, are unique and important, then it opens up all kinds of questions, possibilities, and responsibilities. Albert McClellan said it clearly:

> At times the churches have regarded themselves as Noah's ark of salvation, fortified camps, God's minorities, spiritual fellowships, ecclesiastical societies, temples where God lives, family clubs, and in many other ways. These half-true notions grow out of the experience of Christians in their environment. Most of these concepts are based on an understanding of the church as a place to go or an organization to belong to. These are "come structures" in contrast to "go structures."[11]

23

In the Old Testament, the priestly duties were left to the tribe of Levi. But in the New Testament, the priestly functions became the responsibility of the entire church. Ministry became the work of the entire priesthood. According to I Peter 2:9, all Christians are a part of that royal priesthood: "But you are a chosen people, a royal priesthood, a holy nation, a people belonging to God, that you may declare the praises of him who called you out of darkness into his wonderful light."

All Christians—all of the royal priesthood—need to exercise their gifts, to be involved in, rather than merely recipients of, the ministry of the church. Youth work provides that opportunity to serve. Youth ministry is, in fact, in many ways the perfect opportunity, because it works best when done not by paid professionals, but by the church. And it is the perfect opportunity in another sense as well: it is among the most significant of all the tasks of the church.

✳ THE SIGNIFICANCE OF YOUTH MINISTRY

In *Discipling the Young Person* by Paul Fleischmann, E. V. Hill is quoted as saying:

> So the first thing that I would like to impress upon you who work with young people is that you are the most needed workers we have. More than the senior pastor, more than anybody else, you are at the cutting edge. You are the ones who will insure the kind of leadership, the kinds of husbands and wives, the kind of children that we're going to have in our churches in years to come. So straighten out your shoulders and try not to be too proud, but grasp the significance of the position you are in.[12]

Three out of every four American youth receive no consistent religious instruction whatever. Notice that I did not say that three out of four young people are not in an evangelical church where the Word of God is taught and where discipleship is available. I said three out of every four American young people get *no* religious instruction—at all: Protestant, Catholic, Jewish, cultists, what have you.

24

Here's another fact: four out of five children currently in the educational programs and ministries of evangelical churches today will not be there through the teen years.

These facts tell us, first of all, that we are not reaching enough young people, and second, that we are not holding the young people we *have* reached. We are not reaching kids, nor are we retaining them.

The question nags: How significant is youth ministry? Is it a waste of time? Could we invest our lives more profitably in another form of ministry? I believe that the answer is no. Dr. Howard Hendricks of Dallas Theological Seminary shares five reasons why we must immerse ourselves, *lose* ourselves in a ministry to young people. I intend to convince you of that. I hope by the time you finish this chapter you are foaming at the mouth.

1. Youth ministry is significant because youth are the most spiritually responsive segment of society. Eighty-five percent of all people who receive Christ do so before age nineteen—and the cults know it. (Remember— Jesus said, "The children of the world are smarter in their generation than the children of light.") That's why the cults go for the jugular vein. Their primary evangelistic emphasis is to youth. Sure, they're interested in people my age, too— but only because it's from older people like me that they get their cash. Their commitment is to youth.

In our neighborhood, at least once every month the Mormons come to the door. Very seldom do they send an older couple; they usually send two neatly dressed, polite young men. It is the fastest growing sect in our community. The Mormon Church is committed to reaching young people.

Studies have shown that if we don't reach a college student on a university campus in the first semester on that campus the possibilities of reaching that student for Christ are phenomenally lowered with each passing semester.

The bulk of the people who come to Christ come during

25

their childhood or their adolescent years, when they've not yet attained the pseudo-sophistication of adulthood.

Jim Rayburn said it years ago, and we've yet to improve on his insights. He said that kids will respond to the gospel if we are willing to build relationships, if we are willing to win a hearing, if we are willing to earn the right to communicate the gospel.

2. Youth ministry is strategic because adolescence is the time when the most determinative decisions of life are made. There are four critical decisions made in adolescence that shape the whole course of an individual's life. First, there is the decision of career. How do you plan to spend your life? How do you plan to invest your gifts? We need to help kids decide what God wants them to do vocationally.

There is the decision of companionship. It's impossible to work with teenagers and not realize what a great impact peers have on any young person today. Besides those close and significant relationships with same-sex friends, adolescents are beginning to learn to relate to friends of the opposite sex in a variety of ways, from platonic friendship to romance.

Which brings us to the third decision—courtship. I think we should declare a moratorium on sex education. The big need today is the area of *love* education. Most young people think love and sex are synonymous.

The fourth critical area is the area of convictions—the establishment of your life's ideals. The pressure to merely adopt the values and convictions of the society we live in is tremendous at this age. To me, the interesting thing is not that kids get fouled up—it's that some don't.

3. Youth ministry is strategic because young people still have an entire life in which to live and serve Christ. Once D. L. Moody, upon returning from a meeting in England, was asked by a friend how many converts he had had at the meeting. "Two and a half," Moody responded.

"Two and a half?" the friend asked, puzzled. "Oh—you mean two adults and one child."

"No," Moody responded, "I mean two children and one adult."

Young people have their entire life before them, an entire life to invest for Jesus Christ. Take the time to study the book of Ecclesiastes. For our generation, it may be the most relevant book in the Scriptures. At the end of that book, in chapter 12, verse one, the writer says, "Remember your creator in the days of your youth *before* [before you fall apart at the seams, before you get one foot on a banana peel and the other on a grave, before you forfeit all your opportunities] the days of trouble come and the years approach when you will say, 'I find no pleasure in them.'"

4. Youth ministry is strategic because young people are desperately searching for models. It was Albert Bandura of Stanford who did the most extensive research in this area. He called modeling the greatest form of unconscious learning. The impact you will have on young people comes from what is being caught from you more than what is being taught by you. That's what Paul meant in I Corinthians 11:1 when he wrote, "Follow my example as I follow the example of Christ." There is no question that kids are following you. The question is, Are you following Christ?

I ask kids on high school campuses, "Who do you want to be like?" They respond, "Mister, I haven't found *anyone* I want to be like." Kids are screaming for a man or a woman with integrity. Somebody they can trust. Somebody they can model their life after. Not somebody who is perfect, but somebody who is progressing. Not somebody who has got it all together, but someone who, in the midst of the struggle, experiences the grace of God in his or her life every day.

5. Youth ministry is strategic because youth ministry represents the greatest reservoir of future Christian leadership. Making an impact on the kids who will outlive you is the only way to guarantee the next generation for Jesus

Christ. Talk to missionaries, pastors, Christian workers, leaders in the local church—most of them will tell you that all of the important spiritual decisions of their lives came during their younger years. We have the opportunity to build into the lives of young people habit patterns that will be the essential ingredient of their leadership in the church of Jesus Christ in the next generation.

You may be dedicated. You may love the kids in your youth group with all your heart. You may be willing to work night and day for them, even at the cost of your own health and leisure (what leisure?). But the responsibility of raising these kids up to Christian maturity is simply too important, too significant, to delegate to one person working alone— even you. If the church hopes to survive, it must invest much more of its resources than just one person into this most important of mission fields, its young people.

2.
WHY VOLUNTEERS ARE HARD TO FIND

I've been in youth ministry twenty years and the last two years have been the most difficult in recruiting volunteers. That's partly because our society is moving away from volunteerism. We are losing the grass-roots attitude; instead, we've almost gone full circle back to the English mode, when Robert Rake went about hiring people to teach in the Sunday schools. Our particular dilemma echoes the Vietnam war phrase, "Never volunteer for anything." The church is also moving toward the attitude of our culture: "Pay me what I am worth." Churches are now becoming more dependent on paid staff and less on volunteers.

Lay people are claiming they are too busy to volunteer. And it's true that they are working hard, long hours at not just one but sometimes two jobs in order to perpetuate the success syndrome of our culture. Because more women are working outside the home, "free" time and weekends are guarded more jealously. They would rather pay someone to work at the church than do it themselves. The result is that we are seeing more people on paid staff as specialists (Christian Education, Youth Ministry, Music Ministry, Singles Ministry, Senior Citizens Ministry). I know of one large drive-in church that has a full-time parking lot minister!

People are driving longer distances today to attend the church of their choice. In the past, people would walk to their neighborhood church; today they'll drive 25 miles to a church, driving past four other churches to get to it. But, understandably, they're reluctant to make that drive too often during the week for other meetings.

Some senior pastors seem to be caught up in this same me-centered attitude. The philosophy of these churches is to enlarge the worship service and get on the radio or television, which builds the minister's perception and visibility in the community. Youth ministry then becomes a "bolt-on" ministry and not a high-priority item.

All of these aspects of contemporary American culture have a negative effect on youth ministry—reducing the number of available volunteers and diminishing the priority the church gives to this all-important part of its ministry. But there are other forces at work that threaten volunteerism in the church, too—some of them make us reluctant to recruit volunteers, and some make people reluctant to volunteer to work with us.

WHY WE'RE RELUCTANT TO RECRUIT VOLUNTEERS

When you find a Lone-Ranger youth minister, there's always a reason. And the reason isn't usually that he can't find anybody to work with him—it's more likely that, for some reason, he doesn't *seek* volunteer help. Why not? Maybe because finding volunteers is a lot of work. Maybe because it threatens his insecurity—after all, the volunteers may turn out to be better at it than *he* is. Or maybe he's just too nearsighted to realize the value of having volunteers to work alongside him. Maybe he's too proud. Maybe he just doesn't know how to delegate.

It could be any or all of these reasons. Let's take a look at them in more detail.

It's a Lot of Work

Recruiting volunteers is neither automatic nor spontane-ous. There are plenty of methods of recruitment to choose from, but they're all hard work, and most of us are up to our eyebrows in work already. All we need is something else to do. Recruitment of volunteers is perhaps the most unglamorous part of youth ministry, even though it's one of the most essential. Besides being unglamorous, recruitment can be difficult; not all adults readily respond to the challenge of working with young people—but, then again, not all adults should.

Recruitment has always been a challenge. Ezekiel records, "I looked for a man among them who would build up the wall and stand with me in the gap . . . but I found none" (Ezekiel 22:30). Jesus recognized the difficulty by saying, "The harvest is plentiful, but the workers are few" (Luke 10:2).

And even when we've found and trained these volunteers, it's not time to sit back—the work still isn't finished. The average turnover of volunteers is about 30 percent each year. But don't be alarmed. Turnover among volunteers has always been large. We can reduce it by recruiting people to a ministry, not simply a program.

It Makes Us Feel Insecure

Greg McKinnon, youth minister at First Methodist Church in Montgomery, Alabama, described in an article in *Youthworker* how insecurity entered his ministry:

> One major reason some of us fail to recruit and use volunteers is our own personal insecurity. If we're struggling with a poor self-image, we're going to run into problems working with other adults.
>
> That insecurity may show up in the fear that if I get other people to do "my" work, people will think I'm not doing my job. That fear results from a misconception: seeing ourselves as hourly workers rather than as members of a management team. We're not paid to put in hours; we're paid to minister to young people. If we can minister to young people better by involving other people—and we can—then we are doing our job when we get other people involved.

Another manifestation of our insecurity can be our fear that if we ask for volunteers, we'll be turned down. In my first job, as a summer youth director, I'd sit staring at the phone, afraid to call anyone I hoped to recruit. I'd imagine everyone I called turning me down. Usually I'd put off calling till the last minute, and then I would get turned down—because they already had plans.

A third symptom of our insecurity: uneasiness with other adults. Many of us are threatened by adults, maybe because we can't control them like we can kids. When we're sure of ourselves, we're not threatened by others who are sure of themselves. But when we're insecure, we're always threatened by those who are self-confident. . . .

I remember when, early on in my ministry, my volunteer coordinator of youth ministries expressed dissatisfaction over his not being more involved. This fellow was a strong-willed person who wanted to be given more responsibility. He wanted either to be more involved or to get out of the job. Up until that point in my ministry, I had always recruited volunteers who were willing to sit back and let me run the program. But now things were different. I felt like letting him just quit—but I didn't. I swallowed my fears, sat down with him and talked about ways he could get more involved. In time he became one of the greatest assets I've ever had in my ministry. But if I had given in to my own feelings of insecurity, I would have passed him by.[1]

Some paid youth workers don't recruit volunteers because they feel inadequate. The adult volunteers may have far more biblical knowledge, maturity, and insights into life than the young youth worker. The youth worker may feel intimidated by this older adult. The youth worker may not be as creative or clever as the adult volunteer. But, believe it or not, that may be an advantage in several ways. The more creative a youth worker is, the more he will *stifle* the creativity in volunteers. After all, the volunteers won't feel needed if the paid youth worker keeps coming up with brilliant ideas. In fact, the less creative the youth worker is, the more adult volunteers he will probably get—they'll figure that he needs a lot of help. In that sense, an incompetent youth worker is like a Pied Piper. And besides that, sociologists have suggested that creative people often present their ideas poorly, assuming that their intrinsic merit will be recognized instantly. Now, if you have the misfortune of being creative, don't fret. I'm sure God will still find ways to use you!

Others of us don't trust adults because we're still reliving our own youth. Youth ministry is a perfect slot to indulge in this particular fantasy. One youth worker I knew was a nerd as a teenager and was never part of the "in" crowd. After he graduated from seminary, he found himself working at a church where the youth group was made up of jocks, cheerleaders, and other popular kids. He was well accepted by the group, as well as by their friends at school.

The result was predictable: he began to relive his high school days with the youth of the group. At last he was popular, like he'd always wanted to be as a kid. Yet one of the results of this new-found acceptance by the kids was a corresponding lack of trust in the adults of his congregation. His was a youth-centered world.

Still others of us distrust adults because we don't want to be under their scrutiny. We see the adults as the church's (and maybe the pastor's) spies.

No matter what our reasons for our discomfort with adults, such mistrust will devastate our efforts to recruit and keep adult volunteers. They need our support and encouragement, and we need to spend time with them, give them feedback on how they're doing, and encourage them. But if we're uncomfortable with adults, it's unlikely that we'll put much effort into any of these vital tasks.

I knew one youth worker who couldn't confront his adult workers openly; instead, he was always talking behind their backs to other adults. It didn't take the members of his church long to figure out what he was doing. Once they did, he couldn't get any volunteers.

We're Nearsighted

According to Greg McKinnon's article in *Youthworker*, another reason many of us either don't use volunteers or lose them is our nearsightedness.[2] So many of us just grind out what is needed day by day, week by week, with no goal or direction for the future. This short-term approach to ministry makes it difficult for us to grasp the benefits of involving more leaders.

Yet many of us say we don't have time to devote to recruiting and training workers. One youth worker told Greg she hated it when leaders called her all the time with petty questions. Another youth leader said he felt it was just easier to do it himself rather than try to get other people involved. And it probably is easier—in the short term. But if you have goals for your youth ministry, if you have plans and a direction, then you tend to take a longer view—and it becomes possible to see that enlisting volunteers not only provides a higher quality youth ministry for your young people but also, in the long run, makes things easier on you.

We're Proud

Another reason many of us fail to recruit or use volunteers is our pride. *No* one can do youth ministry as well as we can. We're afraid to give volunteers responsibility for fear that they won't perform up to par. Yet in order to keep adult volunteers, especially competent ones, we have to give them opportunities to move into positions of increased responsibility. There may be many things that we can do better than volunteers, because we've been doing them longer. But if we'll swallow our pride and step aside, the benefits to our volunteers, and in time to our program, will far outweigh the wincing we may do at the beginning. The miracle of the ministry is that God can use people like you and me. I've always felt that if God could use me, he can use anyone.

Pride can also be seen in the guru-mentality and Messiah-complex seen in many youth workers. Some of us, to put it plainly, have an ego problem. We love being on the center stage and in the limelight. Volunteers are perceived as a threat. The volunteers we do recruit feel like pawns in our program; they feel used. It is a pleasure to be used by God—but not by another Christian. Volunteers are not there merely to make us look good. They, like everyone else, want some personal recognition of their own. Some youth ministers, usually without realizing it, even go so far as to take credit for something someone else did. Use of such tactics certainly won't inspire adults to stand in line to volunteer for our youth ministry.

Big egos also keep us from recruiting great workers. By "great," I mean people who are successful at what they do—and who, therefore, draw favorable attention to themselves. Unless we have our own egos under control, we tend to be theatened by someone the kids really like.

When I became youth minister at Eastside Church sixteen years ago, I wanted the youth staff to know who was boss. I had called a meeting with some key high school student leaders and the other adult youth workers. One of these adult workers, Bud Corless, made a suggestion about some activity. I suggested something else and the kids went for my idea. This kind of exchange went on all evening. When the meeting ended, I felt I had established the fact that I was in charge.

Bud called me the next day, and in a kind way explained that I could handle the youth program alone from now on, that he felt he wasn't needed. And suddenly I realized what an injustice I had done to Bud, how in my stupidity and ignorance I had ignored his input. And I realized too that I needed Bud—and more importantly, that our young people needed Bud.

I asked Bud to please stay on and to forgive me. He did. Bud and I worked together for five years as a team. During that time he got so excited about Christian ministry that he quit his job as an executive for Monsanto Corporation, enrolled at a Christian college, and is now a full-time pastor in Bakersfield, California. My ego might have cost the kingdom of God a great servant.

Unfortunately, I didn't learn my lesson overnight. I began to notice that some young people went for counseling to youth staff workers other than myself. *Hey,* I thought. *I'm the youth minister. The kids should come to* me *for counseling.* It took a long time to realize how fortunate I was to have other adult workers working alongside me. Discipling young people is time consuming. There is no way that I could do it alone. I learned that if our group was going to do its job of reaching and training young people, my ego had to get out of the way.

It is a difficult lesson to learn. We must realize, as Paul did, that God is looking for team players, not Lone Rangers: "I planted the seed; Apollos watered it, but God made it grow" (I Corinthians 3:6). We are merely God's tools, His instruments. We *owe* everything and *deserve* nothing. Reverse those two verbs and we lose.

The prideful youth worker—and there are many of us— thinks he is self-sufficient and can do it all himself. He falls into these three narcissistic snares: (1) I can know it all; (2) I can love all; and (3) I can heal all. Maybe those particular balloons should be deflated in the training grounds in the seminaries. Too many youth pastors think of their flocks as armies and of themselves as the generals. Youth ministers at seminaries need to be taught to be facilitators, enablers, supporters, shepherds, and resource people instead of the all-knowing answer man.

We Don't Know How to Delegate

Many of us are poor delegators. We haven't been taught how to share the work creatively and end up *doing* instead of delegating. If you begin by doing it all yourself you'll never discover the leadership potential that exists in every volunteer.

You may feel guilty dumping on others the tasks you don't want to do. You may feel like you are bothering them by even asking. The truth is, jobs you don't get excited about may be someone else's favorites.[3] I hate to type. I know the basics, but I'm so slow and make so many mistakes that after an hour of it I'm downright cranky. I can't imagine anyone getting any enjoyment from typing, but my secretary, Linda, loves it. She can actually feel refreshed after typing for a couple of hours. But then again, I do have a strange secretary.

One danger is that after recruiting volunteers we don't know what to do with them. We don't have specific jobs for those we are enlisting. We did not stop to think about how many we will need and how they will fit in. Marlene Wilson put it well: "Recruiting before designing jobs is rather like trying to dance before the music begins. The possibility of ending up out of step is very good indeed."[4] We must have a clear idea of what our ministry needs are. Determine the number of specific age groupings. List the specific tasks to be done.

WHY PEOPLE ARE RELUCTANT TO VOLUNTEER

All right—imagine that you've overcome all those hesitancies within yourself and have resolved to get some of the other adults in your church involved in youth ministry with you. You want some volunteers! Only one problem: you discover that nobody in your church *wants* to volunteer. Just as you had your reasons for wanting to do it all yourself, they have their reasons for being reluctant to join you.

They Lack Confidence

Volunteers have a terrible inferiority complex. They think professional ministers are far more capable. (If they only knew!) They feel scared, uncertain, and totally inadequate.

Most of us can identify with these feelings. In the Old Testament, Moses understood what it meant to lack confidence. Who hasn't had that same gut-wrenching uncertainty felt by Moses with his shoes off in front of a bush that blazed, on ground that trembled with the weight of God's glory. Moses knew what it was to be afraid. I think all of us at some time have just wanted to run when preparing to face a group of young people for the first time.

When God appeared to Moses in the burning bush and issued the call to be Israel's deliverer, old memories of painful rejection quickly surfaced. Old emotional wounds were torn open. Old fears gripped him, and he immediately began to offer excuses.

God's response was sympathetic but direct. God understood Moses' hesitancy. He assured Moses that he would help him, that he would enable him to do the job. Moses' final excuse is almost humorous: "I'm slow of speech and slow of tongue" (Exodus 4:10). As Stewart Briscoe has said, "That was a funny thing to say because he was pretty quick with the excuses."[5] Again, God, in His love, was sympathetic to Moses' problem. Moses finally gave in, reluctantly.

Moses lacked self-confidence, and yet God used him in spite of his weakness. There is obviously hope for all of us. In spite of our shortcomings, failures and weaknesses, God can use us.

They're Afraid

Most of us don't stop to think about the paranoia that strikes a volunteer youth worker facing fourteen high schoolers for the first time:

- Fear of their blue hair, strange music, and new language
- Fear of running out of ideas for things to do or say
- Fear of the kids knowing more than the volunteer
- Fear of the kids going wild and of not being able to control them
- Fear of the kids not liking them
- Fear of "Once you're in you'll never get out"

These fears are seldom verbalized but often felt. It's important to remember them when recruiting adults. Youth ministry can be like a parachute jump as seen in this brief story by Eugene C. Kennedy:

The Parachute

Research on army parachutists has revealed an interesting truth: Fear is highest for the novice jumper at the moment he receives the "ready" signal inside the airplane. As he steps out of the plane the prospective jumper has already reached what has been called the "point of no return"; he has no place to go but down.

Strangely, it is at this very moment that his fear begins to decrease. In fact, his fear lessens steadily during the free fall, which is actually the time of greatest danger.

The researchers conclude that the maximum amount of fear usually occurs when the novice jumper realizes that he is about to commit himself irrevocably to a dangerous action. As soon as this commitment is made, the fear immediately begins to decline.[6]

You can reduce the fear factor somewhat by sensitivity in how you bring new volunteers into your group. Go slowly and carefully. The introduction process is as delicate as that of introducing your daughter to your best friend's nephew who has just returned from his second year in college. You want to create the opportunity for a relationship to develop without pushing so hard as to destroy the possibility.[7]

They Lack Training

Youth ministers who need volunteers often simply find a married couple and dump the entire program on them. By the end of the year those two will be burned out and never want to do it again. Part of the reason for that will be overwork, and part will be the frustration that arose from not being properly trained in the first place.

Most volunteers don't have the foggiest idea what to do. They desperately need some practical training. I realize that many things cannot be taught in a classroom setting and must be learned by simply being with the troops. But we must offer some basic training to give these volunteers a place to start. This training could be offered as a one-day seminar, or spread out over a few evenings, or given at a retreat in a remote mountain setting. The important thing is to give these new volunteers some handles on youth work that will boost their confidence and ability to work with young people (see chapter 7, "Equipping and Training Volunteers").

ARE YOU A "VOLUNTEER DESTROYER"?[8]

Now that you know some of the reasons volunteers are a scarce breed, here's a test that'll tell you whether you're one of the ones who's making them that way.

1. How often do you check up on people—behind their backs—to see whether they're doing their jobs?

   ____ All the time   10 points
   ____ Most of the time   7 points
   ____ Some of the time   3 points
   ____ Never   0 points

2. Do you give priority to things that make you look good?

   ____ Yes   10 points
   ____ No   0 points

3. Do you tell people how many hours you've had to work?

   ____ Yes   10 points
   ____ No   0 points

4. Do you ever say, "I'll just do it myself; it will be easier?"

   ____ Yes   10 points
   ____ No   0 points

5. Do you sometimes feel threatened by adults?

   ____ Yes   10 points
   ____ No   0 points

6. Are you afraid to ask adults for help because you feel you're imposing on them?

    ____ Yes   10 points

    ____ No   0 points

7. Do you look forward to the praise you'll get for doing a good job?

    ____ All the time   10 points

    ____ Most of the time   7 points

    ____ Some of the time   3 points

    ____ Not at all   0 points

8. Are you uncomfortable around adults?

    ____ Most of the time   10 points

    ____ Some of the time   5 points

    ____ Very seldom   0 points

9. When you give someone something to do, do you:

    ____ Tell them in detail how to do it?   10 points

    ____ Give them specific guidelines?   5 points

    ____ Give them considerable freedom?   0 points

10. How many adults have you recruited in the last year?

    ____ 0   10 points

    ____ 1–2   7 points

    ____ 3–5   3 points

    ____ 6 or more   0 points

SCORING

0–29	points	You have more help than you can use.
30–49	points	You have most of the help you need.
50–69	points	You're doing a lot of pleading for help.
80–100	points	You're doing it all by yourself.

3.
WHO CAN BE
A VOLUNTEER

I am convinced that God works through men and women—not programs—to reach young people. I am convinced also that the inner life of the volunteer is important in determining the effectiveness of a youth ministry. Luke 6:40 states, "A student is not above his teacher, but everyone who is fully trained will be like his teacher." Being a youth worker has more to do with who you are than with what you do.

Please remember, as you read this chapter, that I am describing *ideal* youth volunteers. Don't feel guilty if you don't match up. None of us do. But this chapter should help you to evaluate your own strengths and weaknesses.

WHAT VOLUNTEERS ARE NOT

I don't want volunteers that are grown-up kids. One of the worst things young people can say about a volunteer is, "He's just like one of us." I used to think that was a compliment, but it isn't. Frankly, it describes the youth workers who want to work with kids because, in reality, they're just big kids themselves. They dress like kids and talk like kids. That, in itself, isn't a problem. The problem is that these volunteers aren't able to move kids along beyond their own immaturity. I'm not saying volunteers are not to have some kid in them. The best volunteers are one-third kid and two-thirds adult.[1] Problems arise when this proportion is reversed.

I'm also not looking for chaperones—volunteers who merely view their jobs as keeping superbrat in line and keeping lovers apart. Sometimes youth workers need to do those things, but that's not their primary calling. If you think youth work only means going to church once a week and trying to keep the kids from tearing the building down, then you probably aren't that interested in what they think or do.

I also don't want volunteers who see their task as being the "preacher" in the sense that Webster defines the word: "someone who gives moral and religious advice, especially in a tiresome manner."[2]

So, then—what *is* a good volunteer youth worker?

THE ESSENTIALS

There are a few things I look for in every prospective youth worker volunteer I recruit. I expect each of them to *be available* to kids, to have a *sense of calling*, to *like kids*, and to *be growing spiritually*.

Availability

Young people need volunteers who are willing to be with them. They don't have to be clever or funny or tremendous communicators, just people who are willing to invest a portion of their life in kids. Adults who will be available for kids to talk to. Adults who know how to listen.

Availability includes the willingness to become involved in kids' daily lives and the willingness to let them get involved in your life. Inviting them to go places with you: camping, shopping, or outings with your family. It means inviting them out for a Coke after school at the nearest fast-food restaurant just to talk. Calling them on the phone. Writing them notes, letting them know you were thinking about them. It means being there—just being there.

And that means going where the kids are. Putting a sign over the church building saying "Welcome Young Sinners" will not get the job done. Instead of waiting for youth to come to a church building, these youth workers go to every school event they can (sports, plays, musicals, clubs), making themselves available to kids without pushing themselves on the kids.

Youth workers often feel more comfortable talking to kids in the church building; after all, it's their home turf. But non-Christian young people may feel uncomfortable in the church—especially at first. It's a new, foreign surrounding for many of them. When we go to one of their school activities, *they* feel comfortable and *we* (sometimes) feel uncomfortable. But it's better that we feel out of place than the young people we're trying to minister to.

Some tips for going where young people are: The first time you go to a basketball game at a local high school, take another adult with you because you will probably be sitting alone. If students only know you in the context of "church," they won't know how you will act at their school activities. They may be afraid that if they sit next to you and someone makes a basket, you might stand up and scream, "Hallelujah! Praise the Lord!" or some other unusual cheer.

The first time you go, they will watch you. The second time, if you behaved yourself the first time, they may sit near you but not next to you. By the third time, if they think you are human, they may sit next to you. Eventually, they will start introducing you to their friends. You must earn their respect. Young people need to see how you respond to situations outside the confines of the church walls. They want to know that you are for real, not an escapee from a wax museum.

Effective youth ministry cannot be done by merely being with kids one hour a week each Sunday morning. It will cost you time. You'll undoubtedly have to make some sacrifices. You may need to reevaluate and reorganize your priorities. But it has to be done—you can't minister effectively to kids without being available to them. It's as important as teaching them in the classroom.

45

Sense of Calling

We need a sense of calling. Not a brick out of heaven with a message tied to it, not a desire to duplicate someone else's experience or ministry, but rather a desire to reach out to young people, a conviction that God has ordained us to this important ministry.

A sense of calling is important partly because our motivation for ministry must be pure. Remember James 3:1: "Not many of you should presume to be teachers, my brothers, because you know that we who teach will be judged more strictly." That one thought alone should cause us to pause before jumping into youth work and examine our motives. Has God *really* called us to do this? Or do we have our own, more self-centered motives?

A person who feels called by God isn't in youth work for spiritual brownie points. They have young people on their heart. They are like John Knox when he said, "Give me Scotland or I die." They have that driving compulsion to reach kids. You don't have to use any arm twisting to get them to participate; they're already chomping at the bit. They are willing to do the most insignificant job if they feel it will help the cause. They don't care who gets the credit.

In his excellent book, *Celebration of Discipline*, Richard Foster suggests acts of service that are shared anonymously—for the joy of giving. It doesn't matter who gets the credit. Dale Carnegie adds, "The rare individual who unselfishly tries to serve others has an enormous advantage. He has little competition."[3]

In *Letters to Scattered Pilgrims*, by Elizabeth O'Connor, we read:

> Many of God's flock go about looking at His world through clouded lenses, using church projects to build up wobbly self-esteem, enlisting dependent people to foster their phony selves, passing off a neurotic need for affection as a loving, caring nature, or the compulsion to be ever busy as a priestly concern. Such persons have within themselves all kinds of conflicts

which produce dissension in the groups to which they belong. Their vulnerability, excessive demands, expectations and criticisms make genuine community impossible.[4]

We've all seen or experienced this kind of "spiritual abuse" at some time; we know how deadly it can be. How can we avoid it in the future? How can we tell about motives, our own or other's? How can we tell the difference between self-righteous service and those with a sense of calling? Richard Foster gives us some guidelines that may help:

Self-Righteous Service	*Sense of Calling*
Enjoys the titanic, "big deal" service—especially if it shows on the ecclesiastical scoreboards.	Doesn't distinguish between large and small service— welcomes both.
Requires external rewards, having others notice and applaud.	Rests content in hiddenness. Doesn't fear the lights and blare of attention but doesn't seek them.
Highly concerned with results and reciprocation. Bitter disappointment if results fall below expectations.	Delights in the service itself, without need to calculate results. Serves enemies as well as friends.
Picks and chooses whom to serve. Affected by moods and whims.	Servant of all. Ministers simply because there is a need—the service disciplines feelings rather than vice versa.
Comes through human effort alone—immense energy spent on determining *how* to serve.	Comes from a relationship with the Divine. Serves out of "whispered promptings and divine urgings."[5]

Youth volunteers who have a sense of calling can handle criticism and are willing to accept responsibility better than those who are involved for merely selfish motives.

On April 25, 1980, when Americans had already been held hostage in Iran for 173 days, President Carter appeared on the television. Solemnly, he disclosed to the American people that a United States military team had failed in its attempt to rescue the 50 Americans held hostage in the American Embassy in Teheran, Iran. After the president described the events that led to the aborted mission, he stated, "It was my decision to cancel it when problems developed. The responsibility is fully my own." He did not pass the buck.

Those with a sense of calling are also teachable. They know they don't know it all, but they want to learn all they can to do their work better. They are on the cutting edge. They don't think they have arrived. Mrs. Doolan, who had a great love for young people, was in her eighties and still going to seminars and workshops. When I would ask her why she was attending conference sessions where she knew more than most of the speakers, she would shoot back at me without hesitation, "There is always more to learn to be effective in my ministry." May her tribe increase.

In Acts 18:26 we see this quality in Apollos. "He began to speak boldly in the synagogue. When Priscilla and Aquila heard him, they invited him to their home and explained to him the way of God more adequately." Imagine that—a preacher being taught by the lay people! It's amazing that they felt the freedom to do that, and no less amazing that Apollos had the humility and prudence to listen. He had a willingness to learn.

Volunteers who have a sense of calling are dreamers. They can envision what God can do in and through their young people. They can hardly wait to get up in the morning to tackle that day's activities.

Christopher Wren, the architect who designed St. Paul's Cathedral, asked one of the laborers what he was doing. Not realizing that it was Christopher Wren who had asked him, the worker angrily replied, "Taking this brick and cementing it to this brick—same thing I do every day," and then drearily returned to his work. A few yards away Christopher Wren asked another worker the same question. The second worker, who also did not realize who he was talking to, responded enthusiastically, "Helping Christopher Wren build St. Paul's Cathedral," and then returned to his work with a contagious smile and obvious excitement at the work that lay before him. The difference between the men was that one saw what he was doing as a crucial part of the entire project, and the other did not.[6]

Volunteers with a sense of calling see themselves as working side by side with Jesus as they minister to young people. They have a true sense of the importance of their ministry.

Like Kids

— Want to know how to get my attention? Here's a promise: I'll follow you barefoot over burning coals, hang on your every word, testify to the fact of your wisdom to my friends, and follow your advice if you will do just one thing for me: *Like me!*[7]

If kids sense that you like them, you'll be able to use almost any resource with some degree of success. The number-one question on most kids' minds when it comes to adults is, "Am I okay? Do you like me?" You don't need the techniques as much as the willingness and desire to be around kids. In reality, we minister to kids not in the structured time, but in the casual, relaxed times.

Here's the warning, though: Like kids and you'll get hurt. Adolescents are famous for their ability to disappoint adults. That's part of the risk we must take in extending ourselves to others. But they will also bring you great joy as you become empathetic, supportive, encouraging, and transparent.

Some Christian colleges tell their students to be cordial but not to get too close to the people they'll be ministering to, so that they don't create jealousies or get hurt themselves. The plan is to function objectively, like a general in an army. It all sounds so noble—but, biblically, it won't wash. The apostle Paul had an abiding love with the elders at Ephesus. When he left them, they didn't buy him a set of commentaries, give him an autograph book, have punch and cookies in the fellowship hall, or have a money tree.[8] Instead, the Bible says they wept as they embraced and kissed him because of the thought that they may not see him again (Acts 20:37).

In the movie *The Great Santini*, there is one scene in the park as the son runs after his drunken father, and he repeats over and over to him, "I don't care what you do, I love you."[9] Youth volunteers that are able, or at least willing, to express this kind of love and interest in young people will have the greatest impact on their lives. It means going to the trouble of finding out what their young people perceive as love and doing that to them. For some it might be a friendly smile or hug, for others just a few minutes of listening, for someone else it might just be a scoop of "pralines and cream" ice cream.

In *Junior High Ministry*, Wayne Rice suggests a variety of ways to show you like kids:

> ✱ I have found that one of the best ways to show adolescents that you really like them is to do things with them that are not required of you. After all, they already know that you are going to be planning programs and meetings, teaching classes, even visiting them on occasion. That's your *job*. But when you are willing to give up some of your own free time to be with them, that's different. Only a friend would do that.
>
> You could take a few kids on a fishing, camping, or backpacking trip, or invite some of them (even on short notice) to a ball game or movie some evening. Try taking kids shopping with you on a Saturday afternoon, or inviting them to your home during the week, or hosting a slumber party. These are all good ways to let kids know that you enjoy their company.
>
> Anytime you can give personal attention to your adolescents, you let them know you are serious when you say that you care

about them. Sometimes all it takes is a phone call during the week reminding them of something, thanking them for something, asking a favor of them, or just checking up on how they are doing. I have used the mail in much the same way. Early adolescents, especially, love to get mail, and a personal note now and then helps tremendously to show kids that you think of them more than on Sundays only.

On the other hand, don't just go through the motions. Sincerity is very important when working with adolescents. They do have the ability to recognize playacting and to spot the phony. They don't appreciate a person who is overrelating to them or who takes the approach, "I'm not really an adult, I'm one of you." What is most effective is consistency and genuineness. It doesn't make that much difference what you are or what you do, so long as you are not putting on a show. Sincerity is the key.[10]

Growing Spiritually (Being Examples to Follow)

I want volunteers who will *show* kids what to do instead of merely telling them. Telling is not teaching and listening is not learning. The real secret of a good teacher is what he is— not what he says. Instead of saying young people need to pray, read the Bible, and be committed to Christ, they should see it being done in the volunteers' lives.

Modeling is the key to discipling. The Bible tells us in I Timothy 4:12, "Be thou an example." I think we've fumbled the ball on discipleship—we thought it was a meeting to attend instead of a life lived out in front of kids. We *lead* kids to become discipled young people—not by pushing, but by being an example. What you do speaks louder than anything you could say. Our lives must be worth emulating.

It is absolutely impossible to give something away you do not possess or lead someone in places where you have never been. Volunteers must be committed Christians.

Young people are notorious followers. They respond to the adult volunteer who shows interest in them, like plants to sunlight. They copy people they like and admire.

Albert Schweitzer said it so clearly when he said,

"Example is the only method of teaching." We are to be blueprints for the kids we work with. Their leadership potential will be either developed or squandered, depending on what they see in us.

I learned this principle the hard way. For a long time I would tell young people how important it is to memorize scripture, and they would nod sleepily and do nothing. It suddenly dawned on me that if I wanted them to memorize scripture I should memorize scripture. Positively brilliant! So I memorized Psalm 1 and laid it on my kids one Wednesday night at Bible Study. I didn't tell them they needed to memorize scripture, I merely mentioned how these verses had helped me the previous week.

The next Wednesday four young people came to me before our Bible Study. "We've been memorizing some Bible verses," they said, "and we wondered if we could share them with you."

Could they! Two things jazz me out of my mind. One is when a young person makes a decision to receive Jesus as Lord and Savior. Second is when young people find something new or fresh from God's Word. I get so excited that the kids have to scrape me off the ceiling. I start foaming at the mouth.

Those four kids shared in the Wednesday night youth meeting. The next week 20 students had memorized scripture.

What made the difference? I had started practicing what I was preaching. I discovered that value-changing principles are *caught*, not taught. Christ-centered youth workers can say with Paul, "Follow my example, as I follow the example of Christ" (I Corinthians 11:1).

Growing up in Southern California, I can't remember all the times I have been to Knott's Berry Farm—but one particular time, when I was seven or eight years old, stands out. When we got home from Knott's, my dad came into my room and said he wanted to show me something. My dad was the kind of parent who bought all the educational games for his kids and encouraged their curiosity. He took me into the dark closet in my room and closed the door. I couldn't figure out what he was doing. Then he opened his hand and in it was this glowing cross he'd bought from the chapel at Knott's. He moved it around in the dark and it looked like it was floating by itself. I had never seen anything like it.

My immediate thought was to show it to my sister, Margo, who is three years younger. She'd never really trusted me for some reason, so when I asked her to get into the closet with me she came reluctantly, with a what-are-you-going-to-do-to-me-now look on her face. With great anticipation, I opened my hand with the cross in it in the dark closet—and nothing happened. I couldn't believe it. My sister thought I was crazy and wanted out of the closet.

I went to my dad and told him we got gypped, that the cross was broken. He laughed and showed me that I had to hold it next to a bright light for a while to make it glow, and that the glow would soon fade unless I brought it close to the light again.

Years later, listening to John MacArthur describe a similar incident, I realized that, just like those little plastic crosses, we need to continually stay in contact with God to reflect His love.[11] I am convinced that Satan will do everything he can to stop us from having times alone with God. Satan knows that will shut off our power source. When we try to do youth ministry on our own power, everything soon begins to fade. Burnout is only a few hours away.

Prayer is the major source of power for the youth worker. E. V. Hill says:

> There is *power* in prayer. Much prayer, much power; no prayer, no power. And particularly for those who are working with young people, prayer is one of the most vital subjects that could ever be addressed.[12]

Alcoholics Anonymous and Weight Watchers have one thing in common. They each have a 24-hour hotline you can call from anywhere in the United States. When you call that number you reach someone with an understanding heart and a listening ear who has felt the same urges you now feel.

Wouldn't it be wonderful if youth workers could have an 800 number to another sympathetic youth worker? Maybe someday someone will start one. But remember that prayer is an 800 number to a sympathetic God who cares and understands. He is our real source of strength.

I am looking for youth volunteers who love spending time alone with God. God is interested, understanding, sympathetic, and loving; he is concerned about our families, about our ministries, about our concerns, fears, and joys; and it delights him when we spend time with him. I think of him sitting in an easy chair sipping hot chocolate with all the time in the world.

The essential root of burnout is a spiritual problem. We burn out because we try to do our jobs in our strength rather than in the grace of God. Instead of becoming spiritual warriors, we become emotional wrecks.

David Roadcup, in *Recruiting, Training, and Developing Volunteer Youth Workers* (Standard Publishing, 1987), stresses the vital need of prayer in a youth leader's life:

> A youth leader who is not ministering in prayer is ministering in the flesh. How are we going to change the young lives with which we work? How are we going to bring about the transformation of life that is so important for them in the midst of an untransformed world? It is through prayer! Having interesting Bible studies and exciting socials is not enough. *We must pray, by name,* regularly for the young people in our group. We must pray that the Lord will do things in their lives beyond the plans that we have made. Youth workers who want to be effective in their ministry must pray.
>
> Prayer is not an easy discipline. Prayer is hard work. We struggle with a lack of desire to pray, wandering minds, difficulty in scheduling prayer times, and struggling for prayer concentration. But we must continue the struggle. Prayer is the

major source in the life of someone working with young people. Grow in your understanding and practice of prayer and you will grow in Christ. [13]

Prayer has encouraged me when I've been on the verge of calling it quits. I keep a prayer-time diary in which I record specific prayer requests and the date. In a parallel column I list God's answers and the date they come.

When I feel "down," I flip through my diary and reflect on how God has answered my requests in the past. God's time schedule and unique way are hard to understand sometimes. I receive added confidence by looking with hindsight and realizing that God is in control.

Ask yourself: Is God nervous about the upcoming retreat, youth drama, or board meeting? Is He biting His nails? Then why are you? Whose ministry *is* this?

DEFINITE PLUSES

I like to find volunteers who, besides those essentials, *understand youth culture* and have strong *relational and communication skills, a sense of humor,* and *patience.*

Understanding Youth Culture

According to Wayne Rice in his classic book *Junior High Ministry* (Zondervan), the best youth workers are those

> who can identify with young people—that is, who can understand what it's like to be a young person. Most adults just can't do that. To those who can't, young people seem incredibly strange—moody, noisy, unreasonable, disrespectful, irreverent, lazy, and just plain crazy most of the time. But to the junior higher, there are very good reasons behind all those idiosyncrasies that adults don't like, and they desperately want someone who will try to understand. Without this understanding, communication becomes almost impossible.
>
> Every adult has one very good point of identification with junior highers: He or she was once upon a time a junior higher too—and not too many years ago. And since, in reality, the problems that young people face today are not that different from the problems we faced when we were that age, it seems

logical that we would have a certain amount of empathy almost automatically.

But psychologists tell us that normal adults have a problem remembering what it was like to be an adolescent. They call it "repression," which is something like amnesia. Repression is defined as the "rejection from consciousness of painful or disagreeable ideas, memories and feelings." It is something that the mind does to make life more endurable—it automatically tries to forget, or at least block from memory, painful experiences of the past. Those painful experiences are never lost completely from consciousness; they are just pushed back into the recesses of the mind and never recalled. It's common for therapists to use hypnosis or some other method to help people recall and deal with repressed events.

What does all this have to do with working with young people? Simply that psychologists also tell us that some of life's most painful experiences occur during our adolescent years. Consider the embarrassment and humiliation of the struggle with parents for independence, the times when one was not accepted by the peer group, guilt feelings brought on by new awareness of one's sexuality, puzzling questions from a developing mind, love triangles and broken hearts—the list goes on. No one wants to go through life with all that on his mind. So it is repressed. And that accounts for the average adult's inability to understand young people very well. They just don't remember.[14]

To be effective in youth work it's important to empathize with our young people, to feel their pain and joy. Junior high and high schoolers need to know that we can identify with their feelings, both physical and emotional. The most commonly recurring complaint of young people about adults is, "But you don't understand!" To neutralize that fear, we need to not only hear their words but show that we genuinely care and that we remember similar feelings ourselves.

If you're having trouble recalling your teenage years, one way to awaken those feelings is to read as many books and magazines on youth culture as you can get your hands on. But the best way, of course, is to simply hang around kids. Some little thing they do or say, some look that passes between a girl and a boy, some giggle, some tone of voice, will trigger a flood or memories.

School events provide opportunities to meet students on neutral ground. Plays, concerts, and athletic events all give you time to spend with kids and also give you a natural topic of conversation. Ask questions—probing questions if the situation is appropriate—about their likes, dislikes, and reactions to happenings around school. Listen to the music they are listening to. It will give you a glimpse into the minds of your young people.

School newspapers are an indispensable source of information. If you work with high school students, write their school or schools and request a subscription to their school paper. Many schools have a mailing list of subscribers. If they don't, most faculty newspaper advisors wouldn't mind mailing you a copy if you pay the postage. The insight into the inner ticking of the school is well worth the minimal investment. You may even get ideas from the papers that you can use to base a lesson or group meeting on.

Young people are extremely idealistic; they place unreal expectations on themselves and those around them. They get discouraged easily and begin to be more critical of their parents.

They have a large appetite and love to eat. If you put out three pizzas they'll eat three; if you put out eight they'll eat eight; if you put out a dozen they'll eat a dozen.

They spend a lot of time in front of the mirror. They are very conscious of their physical appearance. They want to fit in, to be accepted and liked. Their peer group is important to them.

Emotionally, they're on a roller coaster. It's either Death Valley or Mount Everest. In the classroom they're great one week and disaster the next. It's incredible! One week they are attentive and well behaved and ask terrific questions. You go out of the classroom riding on a cloud; life is tremendous; you love kids. The next week it's disaster city. You wonder if the week before they had gone home and called each other saying, "Hey, we were too nice last week."

It's important not to blame yourself or take it personally. You think your teaching has gone in one ear and out the other. It's horribly frustrating. But the time you've spent on them hasn't gone to waste; it'll pay off. You can bank on it.

Sexual desires are intense at this age and almost all want more information from trustworthy sources regarding the feelings they are having.

They are extremely self-conscious. David Elkind in his book, *All Grown Up and No Place To Go*, describes the "imaginary audiences" that many high schoolers have.[15] You can see this illustrated at most high school football games. Some kids never look at the game—they just walk back and forth in front of the stands, as if everyone came to watch them in their new clothes or new hairstyle.

They argue for the sake of arguing. Capitalize on that—create an atmosphere in which you *encourage* your kids to argue and ask searching questions. We need to teach kids to question more answers instead of teaching them to answer more questions. Too often we give kids answers to remember rather than problems to solve.

Young people are creative, and they have a keen sense of humor. Two weeks ago, one group "marshmallowed" my lawn. They took over five hundred marshmallows, put each one on a toothpick, and stuck the toothpicks with the marshmallows in neat, straight rows on my lawn. It looked like a miniature forest of marshmallow trees.

In today's youth culture, there are no absolutes. Young people are bombarded with the idea that there is no right or wrong.

The disappearance of marriage as a dependable, permanent structure has caused many changes within families. Many parents are going through their own midlife crisis and are so self-absorbed with their own problems (divorce, job change, unfulfilled goals) that they cannot protect, guide, or support their teenagers.

Families are smaller, and those smaller families are

more mobile (20 percent of the population moves every year). The kids in smaller families tend to be more self-centered because parents are able to cater to the individual needs of their kids.

Another area of concern: In a 1986 poll of 280,000 college freshmen taken by UCLA and the American Council on Education, 67 percent of all women and 75 percent of all men rated "being well off financially" as the number one goal of their life. That percentage is higher than any other group of freshmen since the survey began in 1966.[16]

What's the solution? We can't turn back the clock to a less terrifying time. We can't alter the pace of technological change. But we can—and *must*—provide young people an atmosphere of safety where they are accepted, loved, and listened to. We must protect them from fast schedules and lack of privacy and give them time to think, to be alone, to communicate. We must not demand that young people conform to particular standards in order to be loved.

We must provide programs that encourage friendships, that break down social barriers, and that give kids the chance to know each other. What kinds of programs are those? Small ones, with lots of advisors and lots of service projects or cooperative work projects.

One of the primary aims of Christian youth work should be the provision of great, positive, and good experiences. Young people must be allowed the opportunity to be creative, to play, to be spontaneous, to experience God firsthand.

Relational Skills

"BAKE SALE," said the sign over the door. Joe's mouth started watering. He counted his money. Good—there was enough. He pictured rows of homemade pies. Or perhaps a cake? German chocolate was his favorite. With great excitement he flung open the door and entered the long, narrow building.

Joe couldn't believe his eyes. He saws rows and rows of tables. One labeled "cakes," another "pies," another "cookies," another "French pastries." But there were no cakes, pies, cookies or pastries to be seen. Not so much as a crumb. Only boxes of 4x6 cards. For as you see, this was a recipe bake sale.

As Joe stood staring at the tables, the commotion started. The clamor was deafening. Everyone shouted at him at once.

"The original Blackberry Pie!!" bellowed a fat lady.

"No! No!" screamed the woman next to her. "My recipe is older."

"Both their recipes have been modified," chimed in a third.

Then the hair pulling started.

Joe sheepishly walked between the rows of tables. The shouting continued.

"Pies like grandmother used to make!"

"Whose grandmother?"

"Buy my cookie recipe. You won't be sorry."

"Lemon tarts—the original lemon tarts."

"Old-time macaroons—the real thing!"

An aggressive hustler grabbed Joe's arm. "Devil's Food Cake. Accept nothing but the best," she said, waving a card in Joe's face.

Poor Joe broke away and ran for the door. His head was ringing with claims, counterclaims, demands, appeals, promises—noise.

Once outside he paused to catch his breath. "Phew!" he sighed. "That's no place for a hungry man." [17]

The message in that article by Wes Seelinger is evident: People don't want religion, they want the real thing: a dynamic, moving, creative relationship.

If you and I do nothing more than build significant memories in the life of a high school kid, we've done something. We may not see these kids mature to the place of a Peter or Paul, but we have given them significant experiences and memories that the Holy Spirit can use redemptively—no petty accomplishment.

You can spot the volunteer who's getting close to kids and building relationships by looking in the swimming pool or lake at camp. He's the volunteer with fifteen junior-age kids crawling all over his body. He's spitting out water, screaming for help, desperately trying to keep his head above water, and the kids are having the time of their life, grabbing their counselor's arms and legs and pulling him under the water. She's the one around the campfire for evening vespers with all the kids trying to sit next to her, with kids leaning up against her legs and holding onto her jacket. Why do kids love these volunteers? Because the kids know, deep inside, *Here is someone who loves me just the way I am.*

Young people want adults who understand their problems, viewpoints, conflicts, dreams, needs, and fears. Relationship building is an ability that we practice and work on. It's like typing—it's a skill. Maybe you aren't great at it now, but you can be. You improve as you go along. Some people have a natural ability; the rest of us have to work at it.

Jesus spent a lot of time building relationships. He was always reaching out to people. One of the most outstanding character traits of our Lord was his incredible sensitivity in dealing with others. The woman at the well, the woman taken in adultery, Zaccheus, the Gadarene demoniac, and Mary and Martha at the tomb of Lazarus all experienced Jesus' great capacity for feeling with others.

Relationships enhance our ability to counsel and teach. We have to earn the right to lead and be heard. Kids confide in people they know and trust. On the other hand, young people can feel the tension from people who don't really want to be there.

In recruiting volunteers I look for *likeable* people. I'm convinced that it is easier to take someone who is likeable and make him spiritual than to take someone who is spiritual and make him likeable.[18]

Communication Skills

Teaching. Most adults who are recruited to work as volunteers in youth ministry are willing to do anything but teach. They aren't alone. Moses felt the same way. All of us, as we stand before a group of young people, have had the strongest urge at times just to run. When you think of the sobering responsibility that, as a teacher of young people, is yours for good or ill, my friend, you can easily develop a severe case of paranoia. But remember that you don't have to do all the teaching. If you're not an effective teacher, then search for someone who is—an Aaron. And if you can't find one, then remember that God can make *you* an effective teacher, to His glory. Each of us can be equipped to teach.

We've all, on occasion, had a hard time communicating to young people. Even after years in youth work, I'm still excited about what I'm going to teach—until the kids walk in. Of course, they don't walk in—they kind of crawl or limp in. I have all these great truths to expound, and they're not even bringing Bibles. I pass out pencils for them to take notes, and all they do is chew on them.

Like anything else worth doing, good teaching involves a few tricks of the trade. At a National Youth Workers Convention in 1985, Bill Reif gave seven of them that are particularly helpful in giving a talk to young people.[19]

1. Have something worth saying. And that takes some homework. You have to *study* to be a good communicator. Resist the temptation to get bogged down in administrative tasks; otherwise, your preparation time for teaching will get ignored. I wouldn't think of going on a retreat without having every logistical detail covered, but I'm amazed at how often I will stand up to speak with hardly any preparation and just wing it. If you have little time to prepare messages, then become a master thief–learn to grab things someone else has already chewed through in books or tapes.

2. Speak to your audience, not someone else. Sometimes I'm tempted to speak and teach the way I think *parents* would like me to, rather than the way that will communicate to kids.

3. Know their attention span. The average attention span of young people is from eight to twelve minutes. Don't fight it–use it. Like waves in the ocean, go to the crest, then back off—then go to the crest and back off again. We need to speak like Muhammad Ali fought: "Float like a butterfly, then sting like a bee." Don't try to come on strong for thirty minutes.

4. Have one main point and stick with it. Be sure that you have *one* main point your are trying to get across, *one* objective you're aiming at, *one* specific thing you want them to live out in their life that week. Then let your entire talk work toward getting that one main point across. If your young people leave the meeting with that one idea in mind, you'll really have accomplished something. But if you dilute your effort by trying to get across several points, you'll be less effective. Sure, all of the points you want to get across are important—but if the kids don't remember them, your time (and theirs) is wasted anyway.

5. Use illustrations. If you use illustrations, they should explain the main point. They are the pegs we hang things on. The best illustrations are real-life experiences, especially personal stories from your life, including times when you failed. Giving kids that honest glimpse into your life lets them see you as open and vulnerable. Other illustrations can come from the Bible, or your imagination, or from books and tapes.

6. Make sure your vocabulary fits. Sometimes it's tough to find the balance—you can go too far in either direction. Try too hard to sound like one of the kids and instead you'll sound like a jerk. Use your seminary vocabulary and the kids will scratch their heads, yawn, and daydream. Use a simple, upbeat vocabulary of carefully selected words that strike sharp images.

7. Talk with conviction and enthusiasm. Visualize a room full of kids that are excited about what you have to say. Talk to these excited kids—even though they may not be in the room. When you speak, you don't want to be affected by your kids' attitude—you want *them* to be affected by yours. Be careful you don't reflect the mood of the kids. Speak from your heart, and let the depth of your conviction come shining through.

Bathe every message in prayer. Then God will prepare your heart and your kid's hearts.

Ability to Listen. Being a good communicator also includes being a good listener. I have seen some incredibly clumsy speakers keep kids on the edge of their seats listening to their talks. Why? Because these speakers loved their kids and were willing to listen to them when they wanted to talk.

The most desirable quality in an adult volunteer is simply the ability to listen—and that means listening with your eyes as well as your ears, watching for facial expressions and body gestures. Being a good listener is more important to the success of a volunteer than the ability to give a good talk.

Good listeners are in big demand. Adults spend hundreds of dollars on psychologists who will listen to them in a nonthreatening, noncondemning manner. Are kids any different? Indicate by your attention that you consider me to be a person of high worth. Listen to my ideas with enthusiasm and wonder. Look at my eyes when I talk, not at my belt buckle or the top of my head. Consider thoughtfully my suggestions. (You don't have to do them—just consider them.) Make what is important to me important to you. Rejoice in my victories, be concerned at my disappointments—and I'll strongly consider adopting your beliefs. [20]

Suppose some new young people begin to respond positively to you as you reach out to them. What do you say to them? How do you break the ice? Tim Coop, a minister in Corona, California, says to remember the acrostic SLIR, and you will have a wealth of things to talk about: [21]

S —School (subjects, teachers, clubs, sports)

L —Likes and dislikes (movies, records, food, TV)

I —Interests (hobbies)

R —Religious background

Sense of Humor

By sense of humor, I don't mean the ability to rattle off a lot of jokes. Someone with a sense of humor is someone who is able to laugh at himself, who has an inner attitude of self-acceptance. Having a sense of humor means you can say, "All right—I made a mistake, but it didn't wipe me out." Young people today need to see that failure isn't fatal—and they also need a Christian model who isn't always perfect.[22]

Someone with a sense of humor isn't afraid to let his barriers down. You can become truly comfortable with him. He can relax around young people, and enjoy being with them. He communicates to kids, verbally and nonverbally, that he likes them—and that's a message they've been waiting for.

Being able to see the humor in even difficult situations can ease tension and stress and get you through trying times. For the youth worker, a sense of humor is not an option—it's a prerequisite. Proverbs 17:22 says, "A cheerful heart is good medicine." Remember that youth workers need to be able to apply that medicine to the troubled spirits of today's young people.

Every summer for the last twenty years I have taken young people to Angeles Crest Christian Camp in the mountains behind Pasadena. It takes about an hour to drive the winding, curvy road to get to the camp at six thousand feet.

One summer I was taking fifty-five juniors to camp in a bus. Halfway up the hill, one boy in the third seat from the front started to feel sick. I wanted to stop the bus and let him outside, but he said he would be okay. Sure. A mile later he began to upchuck; my first response was to get him to lean out the window. He did, but his aim wasn't too accurate, and the lunch he lost out the window came back in the rest of the windows behind him. Five of our kids and two volunteers were drenched—but the rest of us could hardly stop laughing. Fortunately, these volunteers had a sense of humor.

Patience

As love can cover a multitude of sins, impatience can destroy months of ministry. It takes only one untimely outburst or overreaction and some young people will cross that volunteer off their list for months. It's that hot-tempered outburst I try to avoid.

When an eleventh-grade girl goes into a three-week depression, she's miserable. And in that pit, she'll probably say some very unkind things about the world, including the volunteer youth workers. It helps to know that in all likelihood that same girl will be happy and supportive again soon. It all takes patience.

Young people will let you down. They will forget the devotion they were supposed to prepare or the refreshments or the decorations or to reserve the film projector. Kids will blow the best-made plans. Learn to be flexible. You have to be. After all, Murphy's Law could easily have been discovered by watching a typical youth group.

We need to be willing to try new and different things when our plans fall through, to be able to capitalize on the failures of the kids we work with. Sometimes God has other plans than we do—better ones.

A college professor who usually became very annoyed at the students who interrupted his work came one day to an amazing realization: those interruptions *were* his work.[23]

This story by Wes Seelinger, entitled "Then Came Susan," is a great illustration of what can be learned through unplanned events.

> Grandmother's living room was large and dark. She kept the shades down so her furniture wouldn't fade.
>
> One day in 1943, when I was five years old, I sat in the middle of her living room floor playing with my toy cars. I had at least a hundred: fire trucks, buses, tractors, everything— even a hearse.
>
> For me, playing cars was serious business. It took at least two hours at a time. The idea was to form the largest possible

circle of cars on the living room floor. And the cars had to be evenly spaced. Precision was of the essence. I placed my toy box in the middle of the floor. Then I took each car out of the box—one by one. When all the cars were on the floor, I began forming my circle. I was very careful. No two fire trucks could be together. No two cars the same color could be together. It was a tedious process, but I was a determined kid. When the circle was complete, I sat in the middle and admired my cars and my handiwork. And since grandmother never used the living room, my circle remained intact for days. I returned time and time again to look at my cars and to make minor aesthetic adjustments—the red pickup looks better behind the dump truck . . . the jeep seems a little out of line, and so forth.

One morning I was sitting in the middle of my circle. Peace and contentment bathed my five-year-old soul as I surveyed my almost perfect toy kingdom. Then came Susan. Susan was my three-year-old cousin. And she was a live wire. Susan took one look at my circle of toys and charged. My precious, tranquil circle was destroyed in an instant. She kicked and threw all my cars all over the room. She was laughing and squealing—I was crying and screaming. Grandmother dashed in to see who was being murdered.

Grandmother later told me I cried for two hours. And she had to rock me to sleep that night. How can you sleep when your world has been destroyed?

The next morning I went to the living room to survey the damage. My cars were scattered all over the living room floor. I began the slow, painful process of rebuilding. But when Grandmother told me Susan was coming over again, I gave up in despair. So when my rambunctious little cousin arrived, there was nothing to destroy.

Susan suggested we take the cars outside. What an idea! I hadn't thought of that. But what if they get dirty? What if one of my precious toys gets lost or broken? It wasn't my idea of playing cars, but I gave in. I decided to risk taking my cars outside. No use trying to build a circle with Susan around. We played outside all day. We put real dirt in the dump truck. We shoved the cars across the front porch as hard as we could. We made ramps, and forts, and tunnels. I even let Susan talk me into crashing cars together. I had no idea playing cars could be so much fun.

A lot of water has gone under the bridge since that day in 1943. I have listened to hundreds of sermons and Sunday school lessons. I have read stacks of theology books. And a seminary degree hangs on my office wall. But I think Susan taught me all I really know about theology—faith is the freedom to leave the dark, musty living room and risk what you love most in the great outdoors.[24]

VOLUNTEERS COME IN ALL SHAPES, SIZES, AND AGES

Even though volunteers come in all shapes, sizes, and ages, most youth pastors have an unfortunate tendency when we need volunteers—raid the young adult class. For some reason we forget that the ideal team of volunteers for any youth group consists of adults of a variety of ages, possibly some grandparents, people the age of the kids' parents, newly married couples, single adults, and college students. Each group makes a unique contribution to the maturity of young people.[25] I look for volunteers that are old enough to be respected and young enough to keep up.

Age, believe me, has nothing to do with your ability to work with young people. I know some sixty-year-olds who are tremendous and some twenty-year-olds who are too old to be youth workers. It has nothing to do with age—but everything to do with attitude. In fact, most youth workers improve with age. I hope you take advantage of your age if you are beyond your twenties. I'm at an age (thirty-nine) when some of our young people see me as a father figure; I'm safe for them. And their parents feel more comfortable sharing with me; I'm their peer. They treat me with more respect. They listen to me.

A Balance of Men and Women Volunteers

The ratio of men to women volunteers should be proportionate to the makeup of the group. One reason for this is that, in one-on-one counseling, young men may feel more comfortable talking about some areas of their life with an adult male—and, of course, the same for young women talking with adult women. And it certainly helps, when it comes to summer camp, to have a large pool of adults of each sex to choose from as camp counselors.

A good mix of men and women volunteers will help attract young people of both sexes. And remember that, as stated earlier, our young people need a variety of role models to watch and emulate.

Involving College Age in Youth Ministry

In his book *The Manual* (Christian Publications, 1983), Len Kageler points out that the average college student remembers very well his own junior and senior high days, and that gives him some real advantages when it comes to understanding and empathizing with youth.[26] This age group still abounds in energy; they tend to thrive as much as teenagers on late nighters and weekend retreats. They can be great and enthusiastic leaders of games, especially ones that are rough or exhausting. Their schedules usually allow them time to be with the youth, even outside the programmed activities.

What do college-age volunteers lack? Usually, the wisdom and responsibility expected by parents of teens. Here's a classic case: I receive a call from distraught parents two hours after their son or daughter was to be home from a youth event. What happened? No real problem—except that the college-age staff person, in driving the teen home, got into a heavy talk. Maybe the staff person even thought to ask the teen, "Are you sure it's okay with your parents to be out this late?" Of course, the kid said yes, and they continued in their meaningful conversation. College-age people need to be informed about the high level of concern parents usually have about things like arriving home at a reasonable hour. They need to be reminded that junior and senior highers don't enjoy the personal freedoms they do. I also try to kill, way back when I recruit the volunteers in the first place, any thought of dating relationships between staff and teens. College-age guys may need to be cautioned especially.

Involving Young Couples in Youth Ministry

In the same book, Len suggests using young couples as youth ministry volunteers as well. These folks, like their college-age counterparts, still enjoy reasonable proximity in age to the youth, and may "relate" very well. They benefit from the added wisdom that comes from a few more years of life experience and spiritual growth. They're more likely to follow through on responsibility, and volunteering for youth ministry gives the couple a chance to enjoy something together. Another advantage is that they provide good role models for teens who are thinking ahead to their own marriage.

> One main drawback with young couples is that they tend to have a baby or two or three. It's nice that these couples are serious about church growth and are personally doing something about it, but two arms full of babies makes youth ministry tough. When I'm recruiting young couples, I usually mention "youth ministry maternity leave," and explain the appropriate ways in which other young couples with small babies and children have been able to serve.[27]

Involving Senior Citizens In Youth Ministry

Yes, I'll admit it takes a special kind of senior citizen to pull this off, but there are some real advantages. Most senior citizens have plenty of time to give to kids. They're available, and many have a large dose of wisdom and common sense. The youth will respect them and go to them for counsel. They are usually able to get away to go as a counselor to camp for a week during the summer or help on an Easter work project. Many have had children of their own and know some of the pitfalls of youth.

Young people in our society are afraid to grow old. The distorted view that television presents of old people is pathetic, and almost all advertising is geared to a much younger audience. Older adults are shuffled off to retirement homes so we don't see them.

Even within the youth program at church there is a tendency to isolate youth from older adults. We sit in different sections of the church building and rarely have any social contact with this older group.

Young people need to be actively involved with older adults, if only to ease the fears of growing old. Senior citizens also tend to be more reliable than their younger volunteer counterparts. They follow through on responsibilities given them, often with a great deal of creativity and a wealth of ideas gathered over a lifetime.

As with any age group, there are disadvantages. Some senior citizens are rigid in their ways and have lost the ability to bend. They can be impatient with immature high schoolers. Most have a hard time physically keeping up with this younger generation. Getting thrown in the pool may not be the highlight of their week. But age has little to do with youth work—attitude has everything to do with it. Find senior citizens with the right attitude and they'll be dynamite.

GETTING REFERENCES

It helps, when you're looking for new adult volunteers, to find out what their references say. The questionnaire on the following pages, which originally appeared in Len Kageler's book *The Manual*, can be used to record references from either youth or adults.

YOUTH STAFF EVALUATION[28]

I feel I know this person:

_____ not at all (then please do not complete)
_____ somewhat
_____ well
_____ very well

I. Public impression (Circle applicable description and comment if you wish.)

General Appearance	Voice	Posture	Facial Expression
Neat	Too fast	Poor	Accepting
Sloppy	Too slow	Good	Warm
Good taste	Good projection		Dignified
Poor taste	Too loud		Serious
	Too soft		Happy
	Monotone		Unhappy
			Scowling

II. Personal relationships (Circle applicable description and comment if you wish.)

Approachable	Unfriendly
Unapproachable	A good listener
Warm	A poor listener
Cold	Too busy to talk to me
Friendly	Willing to spend time with people

III. Relationship with God (From your relationship with the person, respond to the statements as you feel appropriate.)

5—Very Evident   4—Evident   3—Not observable
2—Not really   1—Definitely not

1) Wants to do what God wants	5	4	3	2	1
2) Has a love for the Word of God	5	4	3	2	1
3) Has a servant's heart (not bossy or proud)	5	4	3	2	1
4) Does not have an independent spirit (Not a one-man-show type person)	5	4	3	2	1
5) Has a love for people	5	4	3	2	1

6) Does not allow himself to be-   5   4   3   2   1
come trapped in bitterness
7) Has learned to discipline his life   5   4   3   2   1

IV. Please complete if person has a teaching ministry in the group, such as Sunday school, Wednesday, etc.

YES   SORT OF   NOT REALLY   NO

1) Presents ideas clearly
and understandably
2) Encourages discussion
3) Able to keep things on
track without being rigid
or inflexible
4) Handling of distractions
and/or discipline
5) Able to make material
applicable to my life
6) Seems to enjoy teaching

V. Comment on how this person is a positive (or negative) example to you in:

Relationship to Christ—

Relationship to others—

Relationship to the church—

VI. This person is helping our group:

_____ Definitely
_____ Sort of
_____ I can't really say
_____ Not really
_____ Definitely Not

VII. Any other comments:

4.
PARENTS IN
YOUTH MINISTRY

Many youth workers are convinced that youth ministry takes place despite and in opposition to parents. As Norm Shoemaker puts it in *Grab Bag: Resources for Youth Ministry:*

> I can vividly remember occasions earlier in my ministry when parents would come to me before we left in the bus and say, "What time will you be back?" Do you know what I read into that question? Parents trying to play Joe Detective and find out all the things we were going to do. I was so defensive that I didn't really hear a concerned parent who wanted to know what time to pick up his kid.[1]

We need to communicate with parents. Most youth group activities isolate kids from parents, which sometimes does more harm than good. If possible, try to visit once a year with each parent in their home. Stand around the parking lot when parents are picking up their kids and talk to them. You may feel awkward and maybe a little defensive—after all, they're older than you and probably wiser, and you might be afraid they don't think much of you or of what you're doing with the church's youth. The solution: Ask more questions and make fewer statements. And when you do talk, make suggestions—don't give orders.

David Stone suggests inviting parents to youth activities so they can see what's happening. Have them sign up in advance so you don't have several parents on one night. If you do this regularly the kids will feel comfortable with it and will, in fact, look forward to having their parents attend. Stone not only invites parents to attend—he requires them to attend at least once every few months.[2]

If you try to recruit parents as volunteers, you'll discover that many parents question whether they should work directly with their own teenager's group. They're afraid that their son or daughter won't *want* mom or dad attending every youth event, and that perhaps their own kid will stop attending. And, sometimes, that's just what happens. But the slim chance of that is nearly always outweighed by the positive impact parents can have on a youth program. In the vast majority of cases, it is healthy and productive to have parents directly involved in your youth ministry.

THE BENEFITS

Parental involvement follows a biblical model. According to Deuteronomy 6:5–9, parents ought to be the primary spiritual educators of kids:

> Love the Lord your God with all your heart and with all your soul and with all your strength. These commandments that I give you today are to be upon your hearts. Impress them upon your children. Talk about them when you sit at home and when you walk along the road, when you lie down and when you get up. Tie them as symbols on your hands and bind them on your foreheads. Write them on the doorframes of your houses and on your gates.

Darrell Pearson, junior high minister at First Presbyterian church in Colorado Springs, emphasizes in his book *Parents as Partners in Youth Ministry* some of the advantages of allowing opportunities for parents to exercise that role in your youth group. According to Darrell, some parents either don't want to be responsible for the Christian education of their kids or don't have the time to do it.[3] Yet the biblical view is clear: this is a major task of parenthood. By involving parents in ministry we can introduce them to the concept of teaching their children the faith and show them practical methods for carrying out their responsibilities.

Parents involved in ministry understand their own teenagers better when they see them in a group setting.

Many parents are surprised to find that other teenagers are as unpredictable as their own—a discovery that gives them comfort and hope!

The more parents are involved in your youth ministry, the less unfair criticism you'll receive. For example, I try to have at least a few parents counseling at major retreats. If another parent calls later about a questionable activity at the retreat, I refer the caller to the parents who attended. That way, the questioning (or complaining) parent gets a *parent's* perspective on the activity.

Parents involved in ministry are more sensitive to what youth workers go through. The parents who have taught Sunday school, counseled at camps, or sponsored a youth event, even though they may not always agree with what we do, will respect us because they know from experience what we are up against! Youth work is tough stuff. The parents who have joined us in ministry understand the challenges and are more likely to appreciate our efforts.

Darrell Pearson came across one such parent, named Betty:

> After reading in one of my letters that camp fees could be worked off, Betty—parent of a seventh-grader—came in to talk to me about it. I had really meant that *kids* could work off the money, but she proposed becoming a counselor for the week in exchange for the camp fee. It sounded like a good idea to me!
>
> Betty was a good counselor, able to make mature decisions and lead the girls in her cabin while enthusiastically enjoying the typical camp activities. When camp was over, I figured Betty was perfect for teaching Sunday school. "Not a chance," she said. "Now I *know* I'm not meant to work with young teens. But I certainly have a great appreciation for what you do!" Three years later, she remains my most supportive parent.

Another benefit from involving parents in ministry is the expansion of your resource pool. Add parents as partners in your youth ministry, and you've gained access to a group of people with years of practical experience and knowledge that comes only from living with kids. The parents that minister with me have a special advantage that I lack—they know what it's like to be around teens twenty-four hours a day. We need that firsthand knowledge for a balanced ministry.

And last, involving parents in ministry allows those parents the opportunity to use the ministry gifts they've been given by the Holy Spirit. To deny a qualified person the opportunity to minister because he or she happens to be a parent stifles the proper functioning of the church body. Many parents are extremely capable, mature teachers who can contribute much to the lives of young people.

THE DRAWBACKS

As you can tell, I'm a firm believer in involving parents in youth ministry—but I admit that there are some potential problems. Here are some pointed out by Darrell Pearson in *Parents as Partners in Youth Ministry:*

First, as I mentioned earlier, some teens don't *want* their parents involved. For a variety of reasons, some young people may withdraw when Mom or Dad takes an active role in the youth program. Never have I seen a teen drop completely out of the youth group because of a parent's involvement as a volunteer youth worker, but I have seen some young people upset about parents helping out. In all of these cases, the teens eventually accepted the parents' new roles without major conflict.

I try to avoid that conflict by talking to the kids first to make sure they have no major objection before I give the okay to the parents. If the kids show considerable uneasiness about their parents' involvement, I honor their desires. After all, kids are in the process of establishing independence from parents, and for many, the church provides a positive place for them to have some "space" away from parents.

If, after a few months of parental involvement, you sense serious problems developing, it would be wise to reevaluate the parents' participation. The best approach is an honest discussion with the teen in private. Usually teens end up changing their point of view about their parents' involvement when they've had chances to air their feelings. If the young person persists in his objection, you might limit the parents to a small sphere of involvement or, in unusual cases, you might be forced to end the parents' involvement entirely.

Even though young people want and need some space away from their parents, on the whole they like and appreciate mom and dad. A poll of *Seventeen* magazine readers showed that 93 percent of the females responding rated their relationships with parents as excellent or good. The Search Institute of Minneapolis has released the results of a study on church youth from the fifth through the ninth grades. Focusing on over 8,000 students from 950 localities, the study reported that students looked primarily to their parents for guidance. These studies suggest that young people might not be as opposed to parent involvement as we might think. Some may even desire it.[4]

A second problem you might encounter if you try to get parents involved in your youth ministry is *how* to get them involved. Many parents enjoy dropping off their teen at youth activities—it gives parents some freedom of their own. One of my hardest tasks is asking parents to give up attending their adult Sunday school class for a period of time so they can teach young people.

Here are some helpful hints for getting parents involved:
- Keep parents informed of your need for volunteers.
- Let them know how important their involvement is.
- Especially encourage parents who seem gifted in relating to teens.
- Inform parents that they can be involved at any level that fits their abilities and interests.
- Do not let *any* offer for assistance slip by without some response from you.

A third problem: sometimes you find a parent who's more than willing to help out but just doesn't have the right skills or personality for youth work. Don't dismiss this parent with a diplomatic cold shoulder. Instead, work hard to find a place where he or she can help. There is a place for just about anybody if you plan carefully. For instance, the parent who does not relate well with teens can help with administrative tasks. The key is to simply find the right spot for the right person.

KEEPING PARENTS INFORMED

Regardless of whether or not you involve parents as volunteers in your youth ministry, you must be careful about alienating the parents of your teens so much by not keeping them informed of what's up that they resent what you're doing and wouldn't volunteer to work with you on a bet. Unless you want your youth ministry to die a slow, painful death—and especially if you ever intend to get parents involved as volunteers—you've got to keep them informed about what you're up to and make them feel a part of it.

Newsletters designed specifically for parents are the best tools for informing them. Be careful not to send newsletters *too* often, or they rarely will be read. Church bulletins are good too, especially since the message cannot be intercepted by a young person *hoping* to keep his parents uninformed!

LISTENING TO PARENTS' CONCERNS

One youth worker has a parent advisory committee that meets monthly and offers feedback on his program. Another makes a formal appointment to meet individually with parents once a year in his office. You might try a gathering of parents *before* their children enter junior high, thus establishing a communication network early. Or build a small library of parenting books and tapes, then chat with parents casually when they drop in.

5.
HOW TO RECRUIT VOLUNTEERS

WHY RECRUITMENT IS IMPORTANT
Does this confession by Len Kageler sound familiar?

> I have always been a great procrastinator when it comes to recruiting volunteer adult youth workers. Any time my weekly list of things to do became too long, it was with joy and gladness that I bumped the "recruit staff" item to the following week, and the next, and the next. And so the weeks would pass until the absolute, final, unavoidable deadline would arrive.[1]

In my first few years in youth work (as a part-time youth minister while attending a Christian college) it never once occurred to me to *ask* someone else to assist in working with the kids. After all, *I* was the one the church had hired to do the job. If some other adult had really wanted to help that would have been fine, but since no one grabbed me by the lapels in the hall begging me for the chance to work with the youth department, I kept going Lone-Ranger style.

Fortunately, the realization gradually came to me that the Lone-Ranger approach was not particularly biblical, and that God was calling me to disciple not only kids but also adults who work with kids. I discovered that no one person possesses all the gifts and abilities needed in a balanced ministry. I began to see youth work in the church as an arena in which caring adults could find meaningful avenues of service.

The term "recruiting" is not synonymous with arm twisting. It's not like being approached by an insurance or vacuum-cleaner salesperson. Don't bribe, coerce, or threaten future workers. Recruiting is simply making others aware of the need and giving them the opportunity to use their gifts, abilities, and talents in meeting that need. We are recruiting volunteers to a cause, not a task. Enlisting means sharing a vision. Don't try to make it mean manipulation, coercing people to do things they don't want to do.

The people who are likely to make good youth workers are usually some of the most capable, in-demand people in the church. They're probably overloaded with other responsibilities already. You can't wait around for them to simply volunteer. Ordinarily, you'll have to convince them that they can *make* time to do it. You may then have to help them gracefully resign from other commitments—which may not be as dangerous or potentially explosive as it sounds. They may be currently tied down to tasks that others could do, such as members of the congregation who aren't capable of being youth leaders.

WHEN TO RECRUIT

To be effective in your ministry, you have to anticipate the need for volunteer staff in advance. Often, a new youth minister in a church must play "catch-up" and may, even for a period of years, scramble just to barely cover immediate staffing needs. But the goal is to reach, as quickly as possible, the point at which leaders are being recruited months ahead of need, allowing for growth rather than strangulation.

I've found it best to recruit people three to four months in advance of when you anticipate their actual ministry to begin. My major recruitment for the coming school year occurs in May, and I try to have it wrapped up by June 30th so I'm ready to have them plug in by September 1st.

One of the reasons for recruiting so far ahead of time is that you aren't really recruiting volunteers for youth ministry—not yet. You're recruiting volunteers for youth ministry *training*. If you're going to make effective use of your volunteers, every volunteer you recruit will go through a training program of some kind before he actually takes on responsibilities in your youth ministry. More about that training in chapter 7; for now, the thing to remember is that you need to recruit far enough ahead of time to allow your volunteers to complete their training *before* they begin their ministry.

LAYING THE GROUNDWORK

If you're just entering a youth ministry, make it clear right from the start that you expect to develop a ministry *team*. Some saints, even in churches with several hundred members, fully expect that the youth director will "do" youth ministry single-handedly. They'll be surprised when you tell them that you expect normal lay people to get involved, too.

I've seen promising youth pastors become disenchanted and leave the ministry over this issue—they were expected to be the whole show, and no one else in the church was willing to become personally involved. So, both for the effectiveness of your ministry and for your own mental health, do everything you can before your ministry begins to get this issue on the table. If the board and senior pastor are with you, they can do much to make your life easier by preparing the congregation for your team approach.

One helpful idea is to form a bionic committee—a committee composed of four or five adults who are respected leaders in the church, people who have talents in areas you do not. Because of the diversity of strengths and gifts each of the committee members brings, this committee will be spiritually stronger and wiser than any isolated human being could possibly be. Select, for instance, someone who has an organized mind, the kind whose pencil always has a sharp point; someone else who is an entrepreneur, who is willing to step out in faith and take chances; someone who has Godly wisdom, who not only has knowledge of scripture but also is able to apply it to life; someone who has a sensitive heart, who really cares about the needs of people.

People with those talents are probably so busy now that all they need is another committee to be on. So here's the good news: When you ask them to be on your committee, explain to them that you will never meet together as a group—that you just want to be able to call them on the phone occasionally or drop by their work for a short talk. They are not to be your bosses—they're to simply serve as sounding boards for your plans with the youth group. With their varied abilities, they'll help you think through and implement your ideas. This committee that never meets will also be able to get your ideas passed more quickly and efficiently at board meetings, especially if you can get one or two of them to present the idea for you. You might be afraid of saying the wrong thing or ruffling some feathers at a board meeting—but it's amazing how bold the laymen on your bionic committee can be. They'll champion your case and be supportive of your ministry team. And when a respected layperson talks, the board will listen.

Now you have your bionic committee together, and you're ready to begin the actual recruiting of volunteers— but first, decide *why* you need volunteers and *what* they're going to do. Make sure those you are enlisting have a place to serve.

Most of the volunteers you recruit will eventually be working with one age group of kids or another—so deciding how many age groups your youth group will have should tell you about how many volunteers you'll need. If your youth fellowship group is like most, it will be divided into three groups, based on the age divisions of the public school system of your area: junior high department (ages twelve through fourteen, or those enrolled in the seventh, eighth, and ninth grades); high school department (ages fifteen through seventeen, or those enrolled in high school); and college and career youth (ages eighteen through twenty-four). If your local public school system follows the "middle-school" grouping—sixth through eighth in middle school, ninth through twelfth in high school—you'd be wise to follow suit.

Some churches, usually those with small attendance at youth group activities, put the junior high school and high school age levels together. The leaders think that a large group can be more effective—but that isn't always true. Except in unusual circumstances, don't combine age groups. It's true that young people like to be "graded up"—in other words, junior high students like to be with the high school group, and the high-school students like to be with college young people. The problem is that most young people dislike being graded *down*. In most cases, young people would rather sacrifice numbers to be with those of their own age group.

Some churches combine age groups because of a lack of space—they just don't have enough rooms for each age group to have one of their own. That's a problem, all right—but not a very good solution to it. Let one or more of the age groups meet in homes in the immediate neighborhood rather than combining age levels at the church. Even if you have as few as four or five students in any particular age group, it would be better to keep them in a separate group than to combine the age levels. Even if you must combine age levels for special programs and events, let them meet individually for their weekly meetings. If you don't, you run the risk of losing some of your young people, and you certainly reduce the likelihood that any of your young people will invite friends from school.

If your youth group is larger, you might divide up like this: 7–8, 9–10, 11–12, college, career. Very large groups can be divided into individual groups for each grade.

Now that you know how many groups you have, you have a pretty good idea how many volunteers you'll need. The ratio of youth workers to kids varies from group to group, but try to have one volunteer for every seven to ten young people.

Another preliminary step before recruitment: Be sure job opportunities and descriptions are written out and the training program details are nailed down. It's destructive and frustrating to recruit adults and then have nowhere to use them or no training available for them.

HOW TO RECRUIT VOLUNTEERS

First, let's take a look at the *wrong ways*:

1. Make it sound easy. Tell them that their job can be performed with little preparation without cutting into their free time and personal activities.

2. Talk about your super kids—you know, the ones who carry their Bibles, sing out loud in church, and smile a lot.

3. Push the events and trips. Be sure to mention the ski vacation in the mountains and the celebrity they will meet after the next concert.

4. Show off your books, files, and catalogues of ideas and resources. Tell them you have everything they need to do their job.

5. Tell the story of the kid who turned from drugs to Jesus after a volunteer leader spoke to him. (Don't mention that it happened in another youth group.)

6. Explain that you and the pastor have prayed together for the right leaders and that God has engraved their names in your hearts.

7. Talk about some of the flimsy excuses you have received from other people who obviously don't care much about kids. If they know some of these people, mention them by name.

8. Remind them of the person who said no to the opportunity and who was later involved in a tragic automobile accident (or illness, loss of job, or death in the family).

9. Recruit through your bulletins and newsletters. Let everyone know that you're looking for someone to volunteer, and give the job to the first person who responds.

10. Threaten to quit. Tell people you don't think you can continue unless you get some more help. Then, even if no one volunteers to help the kids, someone might volunteer to help you.[2]

To those ten, which appeared in *Youthworker*, I add two more:

11. Use the "Buffalo Bill" method of recruitment: riding into a herd of buffalo and, as they scatter, looking for the stray that lags behind because it isn't fast or cunning enough to get away—and lassoing it.[3]

12. Telephone someone with the pitiful plea that you have asked everyone else you could think of, and he's your last hope.

If those suggestions didn't seem like practical ways to recruit volunteers—and I hope they didn't—here are some ideas that may prove more useful.

First, in recruiting volunteers it is crucial that we pray to the Lord of the Harvest (Matthew 9:38), asking and seeking God's guidance in locating the right people for this crucial ministry.

It is also necessary to involve the senior pastor. He is, after all, your key communicator. No one packs a wallop with the congregation like this person.[4] What he cares about, others will care about. Ask him to preach on the importance of youth ministry. Ask him to encourage participation in the youth program as a vital ministry for the mature Christian.

Your next step can be a tricky one. There are at least six different methods of recruiting volunteers. Select the one that's best for you or combine a couple of methods, adapting them for your particular situation.

A word of caution: When you first arrive at the church, don't be alarmed and panic if some of the present volunteer youth workers quit. Don't take it personally. Some will simply say, "I'm glad you're here. I'm exhausted. I quit!" That's normal. Just move on and begin recruiting others.

The Public Appeal Method

This is the most common method used to recruit volunteers. Start by accumulating a list of names of potential volunteers. There are a lot of ways to select the names for your list; one approach is "recruitment by ability"—finding and enlisting those who have the personal characteristics to make "great leaders." In other words, great leaders aren't trained—they're discovered!

Scott Koenigsaecker of Moraga Valley Presbyterian Church discovered some of the advantages and disadvantages of "recruitment by ability" in the church where he worked while attending seminary.[5] He would attend the new members' classes, trying to scout out potential leaders. Before he went he would look over their biography sheets, noting their occupation and previous church experience. Armed with the names of those who looked good on paper, Scott would go to the meetings and mingle, watching and talking with those he wanted to see in action. Afterward, he'd make a list of the ones he wanted to ask to be leaders.

The advantage of this approach is obvious: Someone who has already demonstrated potential as a great youth leader has a high probability for success. But there are also shortcomings—if a new member has previously shown leadership capabilities, other staff members and ministers will also be trying to enlist him, diminishing your chances for successful recruiting.

Another problem with recruitment by proven ability is that your pool of candidates may only contain a few people. When Scott was attending the new members' classes, for example, he was happy to discover four or five "great prospects" out of a group of fifty.

A third drawback: You may overlook people who have potential for leadership but have never had a chance to demonstrate it. And that can be a significant oversight—over the years I've found that some of my best leaders have been those for whom being a youth ministry leader was a completely new adventure.

Another approach is to recruit according to "like interest or established relationship."[6] In this approach, you try to match the special interests of the youth with adult leaders who share those interests or who have already established special relationships with particular adolescents.

For example, if the kids in your group are especially interested in football, jogging, rock climbing, surfing, writing, drama, or music, you would look for adults who share those interests. At the same time, you'd be considering adults who have a special relationship with your group members— parents, other relatives, teachers, and coaches.

This recruitment approach has two strengths. First, it assures that each adult leader will have a significant point of identification with some of the students. Second—particularly in the case of those who have a special relationship with students in the group—the adults recruited often have useful insights into the needs and desires of the youth.

The weaknesses of this approach are the assumptions that underlie it. First, it may seem appropriate to assume that adults with a common interest or established relationship with students should know those kids' thoughts and feelings; but in reality this is not always the case. A common complaint of young people is that adults misunderstand them—adults who ought to understand them most, like parents, teachers, and youth leaders.

A second false assumption is that a youth minister could recruit enough leaders with shared interests and established relationships to cover the entire group. Someone is bound to be left out, and that, of course, is always less than ideal.

Third is the false assumption that the youth always want to be around adults who share their interests. Many students are drawn to individuals who have different interests from their own, or to adults who don't know them. They may even be intimidated by adults interested in the same things, because they can feel inferior in their own knowledge or skill in the area of common interest. Such a situation is obviously counterproductive.

Remember: No matter which approach you use in gathering your list, if you only consider people who come to *your* mind, you'll overlook many possibilities. Get more names from the members of your bionic committee, from your board members, from present Bible or Sunday school teachers. The church secretary often knows many people in the church through her correspondence with members. Get names from present adult volunteers or from the senior minister of the church. I've obtained some great leads from the church custodian—and, of course, ask the kids themselves who they would like to have work alongside them.

Look for people who show up at youth and parent-type conferences. Go to the teachers of the retired people's class for names. If you just wait for volunteers to pop out of the woodwork, you may wait a long time—and you may not get qualified workers.

After you've completed your list of names, addresses, and phone numbers, exhausting every possible source, send everyone on that list a letter. (I've included a sample at the end of the chapter; adapt it freely to your own situation.)

Even though you've gathered names from a variety of groups and individuals, there may be several interested or qualified people in the congregation that you've overlooked. Advertise to let other people know about the youth worker training that will be coming up and to inform people of the possibilities that exist for service in the youth department.

Advertise in the Sunday morning church bulletin three to four weeks before you want them to sign up for youth worker training, always stressing that taking the training does not commit them in any way to be volunteers in the youth department. Get the word out in the weekly church newsletter (and maybe in local community papers too), and verbally announce it in adult Sunday school classes and from the pulpit. (As a general principle, announce your youth ministry needs—as well as triumphs and trends—from the pulpit at every opportunity. It helps to keep the congregation informed.)

All of this advertising and announcing of your recruitment process serves an important purpose: visibility. Visibility stimulates and sustains motivation and interest on the part of congregation members, and will result in greater involvement.

When you announce the need for volunteers from the pulpit, don't waste the time of the congregation with useless cliches and ill-prepared announcements. Respect the integrity of your people by putting as much time and care per minute of delivery into public announcements as your pastor places in the preparation and delivery of his sermons. This will give the congregation confidence in the ministry before they make commitments to serve.

Though the pastor will usually be the most effective spokesman for recruitment purposes, even his influence will be diminished by overexposure. The pastor of Christian education, the education committee chairman, Sunday school superintendent, and club leaders could occasionally announce the need as well, if they have the communication skills.

Besides the usual ways of announcing ministry opportunities in the youth department, consider these methods suggested by Mark Senter in his book, *Recruiting Volunteers*:

> **1. Interviews.** Remember, interviews can be rehearsed— and that may give some of your less outgoing volunteers the confidence to share what God has been doing through them.
>
> **2. Testimonies.** In many churches, testimonies of adults in youth work are spontaneously shared within the time normally allowed for testimonies or body-life experiences. Planned sharing in worship services is also effective.
>
> **3. Skits or Dramatic Vignettes.** These work best when carefully planned and tied into a theme that is being developed elsewhere in the service.
>
> **4. Slides.** Close-up pictures (no more than two or three people in each picture) can easily be shown in church services to illustrate the types of ministry happening in the youth department; they can also be used with a rear projection device in the front lobby of the church to illustrate the ongoing ministries of the church.
>
> **5. Video Cassettes.** Try putting a video cassette player in the lobby of the church once a month to highlight some of the

ministry activities of the youth department during the preceding month.

6. Media Presentations. An exciting multimedia presentation—a tape with narrative, music, and sound effects synchronized with two slide projectors—can provide a dramatic, exciting "show and tell" presentation communicating the joys of youth work. If your church doesn't have the equipment to prepare or display such a project, sometimes you can rent or borrow that equipment from a school district or community college.

7. Movies. Christian films featuring the Sunday school or other avenues of youth ministry in the local church can be shown as part of the church service.

8. Youth Ministry Bulletin Board. One large display area in a highly visible location, changed regularly, can become a focal point for honoring special people, posting pictures, displaying awards, and featuring ministry needs. Take the time to do a beautiful, creative job.

9. Pins and Name Tags. Some means of identifying those already involved in youth ministry serves as a reminder to other people in the church that they, too, can become involved.

10. Posters. Whether original or the purchased variety, posters can reinforce the message that everyone needs to be involved in service. (Don't leave the same posters up longer than two weeks; they quickly lose impact.)

11. Opportunity Sheets. These can be attractively typed and distributed periodically through the adult Sunday school classes.

12. Bulletin Announcements. Often the first means that we use to recruit volunteer ministers, bulletin announcements are most effective when used with some of the many other methods of publicity.[7]

When the Sunday arrives for people to sign up for youth worker training, have the entire congregation fill out a training card. (See the sample card at end of chapter.) And it might help to set up an information table in the foyer of the church to answer any questions.

Later, a couple of weeks before the training session, send a reminder letter to those who signed up. After the training, visit those who attended at their homes to determine their interest in becoming a volunteer in the youth department.

Telephone Method

Recruit volunteers by calling through the entire church membership. Watch out for discouragement using this method. It can get depressing. You'll call fifty people before you get one potential volunteer.

One-On-One Appeal

Why do most people do things in the church? Because someone asked them personally—sometimes twice. That's the principle behind one-on-one appeal. More effective than the public appeal method and the telephone method, the one-on-one appeal can also be used to follow up after public appeal.

It's hard to enlist volunteers in any large collection of people. It's harder to find two volunteers in a crowd of three hundred people, for instance, than in a group of five people. Many ministers solve this problem by thinking of their congregation not as two hundred or three hundred or four hundred members, but rather as a congregation of groups, classes, circles, choirs, and other organizations. Each one of these face-to-face groups is a potential source of volunteers— and it's much easier to enlist five volunteers from an adult Sunday school class of twenty or a choir of thirty members than to recruit five volunteers out of a large congregation.[8]

Many youth workers approach prospective volunteers cold, with a "Hey—we need more volunteers in our youth program. Think you can help?" And then they wonder why no one says yes. Enlisting volunteers is a little like courting: The approach is everything. You can't just come out of nowhere with a request for help and expect to win the volunteer. You have to *prepare* your prospects.

An important part of that preparation is to *plant thoughts in people's minds* before you actually approach them. After they have done something with a group of kids, mention that you feel they are really gifted with kids. Ask them questions like:

"Have you ever thought about teaching?" or, "What do you think your ministry is going to be during the coming year?"

In approaching the prospect, everything you do needs to be surrounded in love and bathed in prayer. When Jesus selected the twelve in Luke 6:12, he prayed all night before naming the disciples. It is also significant that He enlisted all twelve in person, not on the phone, not through a third party, and not in the hallway between Sunday school and church. Pray for wisdom and sensitivity. Use your common sense, experience, and intuition.

Recruitment interviews need to be done face-to-face, eyeball-to-eyeball, and in private. I recommend the prospective volunteer's home. Telephone interviews or discussions in crowded hallways seldom allow for accurate perceptions of the volunteer. You may miss nonverbal cues; you may be reluctant to ask particular questions because you're not sure who else is listening to the conversation. Besides, if your prospective volunteer doesn't have time for a personal interview, he'll probably not find the time to tend to other ministry responsibilities either.

Don't just drop in to interview your prospect—make an appointment. This is too important to be treated casually. Visit them when they can give you full attention. And when you call to set up the appointment, don't call at a time they'll be reluctant to speak on the phone—at dinner time, for instance, or, if you're calling a basketball fan, when the NBA finals are on television. Obviously, it's important to know something about each prospect before you go to his home. Sometimes it helps to take another person along with you— possibly another volunteer. It also helps to take brochures, schedules, or other printed material to put into their hands. It seems to have a calming effect.

During the interview, don't downplay the required commitment. Don't say, "It will hardly take any time. It's really not much." Be honest and realistic. Tell them what you expect. Give them a written job description.

And remember this: The interview is more than just a time to give information to the prospect and try to persuade him to join up. It's also your chance to find out enough about the prospect to tell whether he'd be a useful addition to your volunteer staff. Mark Senter recommends that you ask the prospect for information in seven areas:

1. Testimony. "Describe your relationship with the Lord and where you are in your Christian walk."

2. Training. "What classes and seminars have you taken that have sharpened your youth ministry skills? What books, tapes, and films or videotapes have been the most useful to you?"

3. Experience. "What experience have you had in ministry?" (Even if the prospect may have no background in youth ministry, it is helpful to know what other ministry experience he has had.)

4. Special Interests. "What do you enjoy doing on vacations or in your spare time?" (Ask about hobbies, crafts, sports, and skills, as well as other talents that may assist in ministry.)

5. Expectations. "What would you hope to get out of your volunteer ministry?" (After you've found this out, try to make sure that these expectations will be met. Choose this volunteer's placement in your staff with these expectations in mind, and check with him frequently throughout the year to find out whether he's satisfied.)

6. Fears. "What causes you the greatest feelings of apprehension as you contemplate youth ministry?" (Two of the most common fears are being unable to maintain discipline among the kids and being "trapped" in the job because no replacements are available. Assure the volunteer that he'll get all the help he needs—and then make sure he does.)

7. Preferences. "In what capacity and with what age-group would you like to minister? What would be your second choice?"[9]

Recruit volunteers to a *ministry,* not a *program.* Program-centered ministries can use people for as little as a couple of hours a week for three months. Relationally-oriented ministry takes more time—sometimes a lifetime. Your goal should be to develop a group of long-term servants who love kids and want to work with them. Before your prospects can really understand what is being asked of them, they need to know that. I bring a copy of our philosophy of ministry and lead them through it—and most of them appreciate that. They're beginning to get the impression, if they don't have it already, that the ministry being presented to them has some depth.

Explain to your prospects what others like them have found most rewarding in similar service, as well as what others have found difficult, discouraging, or frustrating. Anticipate what objections they might have, and be prepared to answer them. Give them the opportunity to ask any questions, listen as they talk, giving them your full attention. In leaving, thank them for allowing you to share your needs; tell them you will call in about a week.

I never press potential volunteers for a decision that first night. I give them some breathing room—a chance to pray and think about it, to talk it over with their family. The purpose of the interview is not to extract a commitment from the prospect. It is to confirm his interest in young people and his desire to personally help them, to explain how the church's ministry can provide an opportunity to do that, to show how and why the individual or couple can fit in, to offer an opportunity to observe the troops in action (without making a commitment), to explain what training would be offered, and to provide whatever else the prospect needs in order to reach a decision.

If, after a period of prayer and reflection, your potential volunteer's decision is no, allow him to say it gracefully. Don't use guilt or pity to try and coerce him into reconsidering. It's not unusual for youth workers to try to shame adults into working with youth—and some people will volunteer out of a sense of guilt. To others, service becomes a way to pay a debt to society or to God. Manipulation, through guilt or other means, isn't scriptural and is counterproductive in the long run.

It's far wiser to accept your prospect's no—but first,

determine what that no means. Prospects may decline a specific request, but that doesn't necessarily mean they don't want to be involved at all. Are they objecting to the job? Are they objecting to the leader of the particular job? If you don't overreact to their refusal and if you allow them to talk about it, their true objection will eventually become clear.

A recent article in *Leadership Journal* pointed out that "no" doesn't always mean no. It may mean "No, not now"—meaning the individual may be willing to help later. It may also mean "Who, me? I could never do that!" If that's the case, maybe you've offered the prospective volunteer too much responsibility. Try offering him a simpler opportunity.

No may also mean you've made it sound as if they will never be able to get out; try offering an opportunity that ends at a specific date.

No may mean that your prospective volunteer doesn't want to do it alone—but would be willing to be part of a team of three or four handling the same task. Find a few more prospects and match them up.

And finally, remember that the opportunity you're offering may appear far more complicated and demanding to the prospective volunteer than it does to the person seeking volunteers. Recruiting several people for a workshop, a seminar, or a series of training classes may solve that problem—the training may make youth ministry seem more manageable to your volunteers, and afterwards they may be willing to tackle it.[10]

This approach is especially useful in those congregations that are seeking volunteers from that huge number of energetic, committed, highly educated, enthusiastic, inexperienced, eager, active, and creative adults born during the late 1940s and the 1950s. Many of these adults are accustomed to some type of formal training experience before taking on a new responsibility.

So when they say yes, don't tie them down immediately to teach, counsel, or be responsible for the program. First, let them observe. Invite them to learn with on-the-job training. Don't grab them in a hallway and thrust a quarterly in their hands. Have them come to youth activities to watch. In a relay race, the hand-off is the most nerve-wracking part. It is crucial that the second runner has the baton firmly in hand before the first runner lets go. Youth ministry is far more important than a track meet, so we must be sure our volunteers are ready before we hand their part of the program to them.

Try to give prospective volunteers the opportunity to visit and observe the age group they are considering for one to three months before you ask them to decide. Some adults like to be around kids individually or in small groups, but they find the activity (and noise) level of a large group intolerable. To grab a person on Wednesday and send him into the junior-high class as the teacher beginning the next Sunday might be necessary once every millennium, in an hour of desperate need, but it's far wiser to allow your prospective volunteers to observe the group and the context in which they would work and decide whether they'd fit.

Make sure that they understand that, at least at first, you won't be expecting them to lead anything. "Are you expecting me to lead the Bible Study?" they'll ask. Assure them that you aren't, that you just want them to *come* to the Bible Study, to be there for moral support, to watch how it goes, to get to know the kids. After they've been coming a few weeks, ask them what they think—whether the discussions are relevant, how they respond to the kids, and so on. If they still seem positive about working with the group, try some small-group activities in your meetings and let the potential volunteers lead some of the discussion groups—with questions you type out ahead of time, so they know they won't have to think of questions off the top of their head. See the progression? In a few months you may be able to give those volunteers the entire Bible Study and move on to new projects.

Volunteers Recruiting Volunteers

Those volunteers who oversee other volunteer staff deserve—and need—special attention. These are brave folks who have an entrepreneurial spirit. They're willing to take leadership, to be held accountable, to motivate, to help recruit. I know a volunteer is ready to recruit other volunteers when he tells me he thinks about his ministry while lying awake at night, or in the shower, or when jogging. That tells me the ministry has become part of him, and that he probably has all kinds of ideas about how the ministry could be improved or advanced.

In general, volunteers recruit other volunteers better than paid staff do. It isn't hard for prospective volunteers to say no to paid staff. It's much harder for them to say no to another volunteer. After all, lay people in the congregation look at paid staff as being *paid* to be good. Lay people are good for nothing! (Sorry about that!)

When a volunteer speaks to prospective volunteers about working with youth, he can speak firsthand about the demands, the joys, the disappointments, the satisfaction. He knows what it's like to have a job outside of church, and how hard it is to squeeze extra hours out of the week to serve in a ministry. If anyone can empathize with the fears of prospective volunteers, it's him. Use the volunteers you already have to help you recruit others.

Getting the Kids Involved[11]

No matter which method you use to recruit volunteers, check out the feelings of your youth group about the prospective helper. If your members don't want him, you're probably heading for trouble. You may want to bring the adult before the group for an interview. You might bring the adult to a group meeting and explain to the group that he is thinking about becoming a sponsor and would like to check things out first. That way, both the youth and the prospective sponsor have the chance to get to know each other before you ask either to decide.

The biggest question a potential youth volunteer has is, "Do the kids want me?" They know *you* want them, but they don't know whether the kids will. What could be more frightening or threatening for an adult than the prospect of standing for the first time before a group of kids who may not like you and may not want you around? For many of us, it's like being thrown back into the insecurity of our *own* adolescence again.

If your prospective volunteers are bothered by this fear, here's a suggestion that will work wonders: have the youth group make an appointment to visit the people you're trying to recruit. If the kids are willing to give this person a shot at being one of their youth sponsors, have them go to the potential volunteer's home *en masse* (anywhere from five to fifty kids—enough that the recruit gets the impression that most of the kids want him). The potential volunteer may be a bit surprised to find fifty kids on his doorstep, but when they ask him to help in their youth program his doubts about his welcome there will be eliminated. Besides, who could possibly turn down a group of energetic, enthusiastic young people?

Getting Recommendations from Church Leadership

When a potential volunteer hears that the church's ruling body or senior minister has recommended him as a youth worker, his motivation to participate soars. The minister or church board may not make any recommendations on their own—but if *you* raise the issue, they'll probably come up with some names. If not, they'll at least respond to your own list of names with their commendations. In fact, it's always a good idea to keep the church board and senior pastor informed of your recruiting activities and to show them your master list of prospects. Not only does that give you added fuel in your discussions with the prospects themselves ("Pastor Jones and the whole church board agreed that you'd be *great* with the junior-high group!"), but it also ensures that the board won't feel that you're pulling something behind their back, benefiting your part of the church's ministry at the expense of other parts.

Eastside Christian Church

2505 Yorba Linda Blvd., Fullerton, CA 92634-4178   P.O. Box 4178   Phone (714) 871-6844

STAFF
Ben Merold, *Senior Minister*
Murray Hollis, *Assoc. Minister*
Nancy Rankin, *Secretary*

CHRISTIAN EDUCATION
Ralph Robson, *Minister*
Gary Lankford, *Assoc. Minister*
Gina Hanley, *Secretary*

YOUTH MINISTRY
Les Christie, *Minister*
Roger Worsham, *Assoc. Minister*
Arty VanGeloof, *Assoc. Minister*
Linda Merold, *Secretary*

MUSIC MINISTRY
Tim Neuenschwander, *Minister*
Karla Ross, *Associate*
Dana Morris, *Associate*
Pat Vansickel, *Secretary*

PASTORAL CARE
Lester Ragland, *Minister*

**BUSINESS
ADMINISTRATOR**
Sterling Fox

MISSIONS
Sheldon Welch, *Minister*
Israel Martinez, *Hispanic Ministry*
Rlea Butler, *Secretary*

MEDIA MINISTRY
John Schmidt, Jr.

HOME BIBLE STUDIES
Greg Tucker

**MAINTENANCE
SUPERVISOR**
Jim Knight

ACCOUNTANT
Diana Erskine

PUBLICATIONS
Kim Osness

GENERAL OFFICE
Ruth Cloer
Helen Alley

DEAF MINISTRY
Stacey Tabak

**EASTSIDE CHRISTIAN
SCHOOL**
David Schoen,
Assoc. Min. Christian Ed.
Robert Lozano,
Assoc. Min. Christian Ed.
Ann Thornton, *Secretary*
(714) 879-2187

PRE-SCHOOL
Arlene Claussen, *Director*
(714) 525-2442

**HELPING HANDS
SCHOOL FOR
DEVELOPMENTALLY
DISABLED**
Jessie Ohm, *Director*
(714) 871-5855

May 5, 1986

Hallelujah! Praise the Lord! (And any other theologically oriented exclamatory phrases.) Your name has been handed to me as one who just might be interested in working with God's kids through our great Jr. High-College age youth program. That's exciting; well, it's exciting to me because we need some Christian folks to help us in some of our youth activities.

Who gave me your name? I'll never tell for fear you might attempt some drastic retaliatory measures against them!

Seriously, your name was mentioned to me as one who has the ability and quite possibly the interest in working with our youth. That's good for two reasons: First, because we need you; and second, because you need us. Yes, you need an avenue of service if you don't already have one.

Do you? Are you actively serving Christ in some way? Well, whether you are or not, I have your name on my list and I'm sure praying that you will consider the investment of some of your life in the lives of some of God's kids here at Eastside Christian Church, so that our church and God's kingdom might have a bright and promising future.

I will be offering a training course on how to be a youth worker. It will be offered at two different times. You may choose the one which is most convenient for you. One will be offered on Saturday, June 7, from 9:00 a.m. to 1:00 p.m. or you may take the training on Sunday, June 8, from 1:30 p.m. to 5:30 p.m. This training does not obligate you to be a youth worker in any way. It only informs you of the opportunities in a variety of areas.

Youth work is a very unique ministry which involves youth and adults working together in such a way that blesses the lives of both. Thanks for the time. I hope you're interested.

Sincerely,

Les J. Christie

Les J. Christie

P.S.   On Sunday, June 1, the entire church will have the
       opportunity to sign up for the training. Please
       sign up at that time.

The Youth Department's Sponsor/Teacher Training Seminar

Today is the day to sign up for the training that will be offered next Saturday, June 7, from 9:00 a.m. - 1:00 p.m. and Sunday, June 8, from 1:30 p.m. - 5:30 p.m. (choose one).

➤ existing sponsors and teachers

➤ adults interested in helping our growing youth group

➤ parents and interested adults that want to know more about our youth program

The training will be taught by Les, Ralph, Roger, and Arty. Taking the training does not commit you in any way to be a teacher or sponsor in our Junior High, High School, or College-Career programs.

Please fill out the information below and turn it in with your silent roll call card at the end of this service, or give it to one of the ministers.

Name_____

Address_____

City_____Zip_____

Telephone_____

Eastside Christian Church

2505 Yorba Linda Blvd., Fullerton, CA 92634-4178   P.O. Box 4178   Phone (714) 871-6844

STAFF
Ben Merold, *Senior Minister*
Murray Hollis, *Assoc. Minister*
Nancy Rankin, *Secretary*
CHRISTIAN EDUCATION
Ralph Robson, *Minister*
Gary Lankford, *Assoc. Minister*
Gina Hanley, *Secretary*
YOUTH MINISTRY
Les Christie, *Minister*
Roger Worsham, *Assoc. Minister*
Arty VanGeloof, *Assoc. Minister*
Linda Merold, *Secretary*
MUSIC MINISTRY
Tim Neuenschwander, *Minister*
Karla Ross, *Associate*
Dana Morris, *Associate*
Pat Vansickel, *Secretary*
PASTORAL CARE
Lester Ragland, *Minister*
BUSINESS ADMINISTRATOR
Sterling Fox
MISSIONS
Sheldon Welch, *Minister*
Israel Martinez, *Hispanic Ministry*
Rlea Butler, *Secretary*
MEDIA MINISTRY
John Schmidt, Jr.
HOME BIBLE STUDIES
Greg Tucker
MAINTENANCE SUPERVISOR
Jim Knight
ACCOUNTANT
Diana Erskine
PUBLICATIONS
Kim Osness
GENERAL OFFICE
Ruth Cloer
Helen Alley
DEAF MINISTRY
Stacey Tabak
EASTSIDE CHRISTIAN SCHOOL
David Schoen,
Assoc. Min. Christian Ed.
Robert Lozano,
Assoc. Min. Christian Ed.
Ann Thornton, *Secretary*
(714) 879-2187
PRE-SCHOOL
Arlene Claussen, *Director*
(714) 525-2442
HELPING HANDS SCHOOL FOR DEVELOPMENTALLY DISABLED
Jessie Ohm, *Director*
(714) 871-5855

June 2, 1986

Dear Potential Adult Youth Volunteer:

I am so glad you will be taking the training this weekend. We have over 80 adults signed up from Eastside and a few adults from four other churches. We will have 60 at the Saturday Seminar. The training starts at 8:30 a.m. sharp. We will have coffee, tea, orange juice, donuts, and cinnamon rolls available from 8:30-9:00 a.m. We will meet in room #111 (Chapel in new building). The Saturday training will end at 1:00 p.m.

We have over 40 attending on Sunday starting at 1:30 p.m. sharp. We will have a break in the middle with chips and dip and small sandwiches. The Sunday session will end at 5:30 p.m.

Taking the training does not in any way commit you to work in our youth department at Eastside. I hope the training will be helpful to your life, as well as any form of ministry you might have. I'll look forward to seeing you in a couple of days.

Your Youth Minister,

Les J. Christie

LJC:llm

P.S. There will be nursery care available.

ADULT VOLUNTEER YOUTH WORKER

Name: _____

Address: _____

_____

Telephone: _____

<table>
<tr><td>Map to Potential
Youth Worker's Home</td><td>Potential Youth
Worker's Picture</td></tr>
</table>

I would like to work with the following age-group:

_____ Junior High   _____ High School   _____ College

I would like to work in the following areas with this age group:

Addressing	Tennis	Deaf Ministry
Afterglows	Volleyball	Drama
Athletics:	Auto Repair	Evangelism
Aerobics	Backpacking/Hiking	Folding/Filing
Baseball	Bell Choir	Fund Raising
Basketball	Bible Bowl	Guitar
Bowling	Bicycle Trips	Home Bible Study
Canoeing	Bus Driver	Hospital/Headliners
Football	Camps/Retreats	Missions:
Karate	Canoe Trips	Haiti
Lifesaving	Carpentry	Inner City
Repelling	Clown Ministry	Mexico
Sailing	Convalescent Home	Multi-media
Swimming	Cooking	Orchestra

105

Painting
Photography
Prayer
Preachers
Publicity
Puppets/Muppets
Senior Citizens

Sewing
Singing
Ski Trip
  Water   Snow
Spanish
Socials

Sunday School
Teacher
Telephoning
Transportation
Typing
Youth Choir
Youth Paper

I will loan my:

Boat
Cabin
Computer

Home
Pickup Truck
Motor Home

Slide Projector
Swimming Pool
VCR

6.
WHAT DOES A VOLUNTEER DO?

One of the first questions your volunteers will have—probably before they've even agreed to be volunteers—is: "What am I going to be doing?" They're afraid they'll end up doing something they won't like or that they're not good at. They want to know whether you expect them to drive the bus, lead the singing, or evangelize kids at the local high school.

The real answer to their question isn't as easy as just saying, "We need you to lead a Bible study for junior-high kids." It's important that your volunteers understand what they're *really* doing with the kids in your youth group. Sure, it's important for them to know whether they're going to plan the retreat or prepare the meals—but those day-to-day responsibilities will probably change from month to month anyway. What's more important is to understand what the needs are in the lives of the kids they're working with, and to know how to best serve those needs. And all of the kids in our youth groups, if they're to mature as Christians, have these two needs: to be given real responsibility, and to be allowed to fail at it.

GIVE YOUNG PEOPLE REAL RESPONSIBILITY

The ultimate goal of youth ministry is to bring young people to maturity in Christ—to prepare, disciple, and train them to serve God with their lives. One of the most effective methods for accomplishing this goal is to give youth real responsibility. By *real responsibility* I mean tasks that stretch them physically, socially, mentally, and spiritually, so that they "dream dreams and see visions" of what God can do through their lives.

This concept is as old as Scripture: "It is good for a man to bear the yoke while he is young" (Lamentations 3:27). A yoke was normally made for two animals. In this verse, bearing the yoke expresses the idea of working alongside others who are performing similar tasks and striving for similar goals. Learning to handle burdens, tasks, and responsibilities helps prepare young people for life.

Too many young people in the church suffer from spiritual constipation. They go to every Bible study and worship service offered. They are constantly taking in, but never giving anything out. That's not a healthy condition in the physical world, and it isn't healthy in the spiritual world either. We must provide opportunities for ministry and service if we want to develop the leadership potential in young people.

In most youth groups the only significant service opportunities offered are for young people who can either speak or sing. These kids can give devotions (Bible studies or testimonies) or present some type of special music (solos, choir, song leading). Those opportunities are great for preparing young people to be pastors, teachers, and song leaders. But what about all the young people who have talents in other areas? What are our youth groups doing to develop the future Christian filmmakers, the future editors and writers of Christian magazines and books, the future Christian actors, seminary professors, missionaries, nurses, doctors, computer programmers, auto mechanics, plumbers, and electricians?

Several years ago in our youth group, we started a Christian filmmakers team consisting of a few of our high schoolers. They made short, 8mm films. One was called "Jonah Meets Jaws"—which gives you an idea of the fine quality of these films. Still, they got the message across—and more importantly, they gave opportunities for developing leadership potential. Out of that group came a young man named John Schmidt, who has since made several award-winning Christian films including *Super Christian, Kevin Can Wait, The Greatest Story Never Told, The Wait of the World,* and *Super Christian II.*

Give young people a vision of how God can use them, and they'll do things beyond our wildest dreams. Consider this list:

Addressing
Auto Repair
Backpacking/Hiking
Bell Choir
Bible Memorization
Bicycle Trips
Camps/Retreats
Canoe Trips
Carpentry
Clown Ministry
Convalescent Home
Cooking
Deaf Ministry
Drama
Evangelism
Folding/Filing
Fund Raising
Guitar
Home Bible Study
Hospital/Headliners

Missions:
   Haiti
   Inner City
   Mexico
Multimedia
Orchestra
Painting
Photography
Prayer
Publicity
Puppets/Muppets
Senior Citizens
Sewing
Singing
Spanish
Sunday School Teacher
Telephoning
Transportation
Typing
Visitation
Youth Choir
Youth Paper

All of those are valid areas of ministry for the kids in your youth group. But don't try to offer all of them at once. Try one new ministry, "Puppets" for example, for six weeks. If none of your young people are excited about it, drop it and try another.

You'll find adults in your church who have the talent and willingness to train young people for many of these ministries, giving them a ministry with youth and opening new avenues of service for the young people. And you undoubtedly have adults in your church who have skills other than those listed. How about plumbers or electricians? They could teach young people a skill while ministering to people in the church and community who need their services (for example, elderly church members who need home repairs done). Such ministry opportunities help young people feel successful while developing the leadership potential God has given them.

In *any* of these group projects, the adult volunteer leaders assist, but do not run, the projects. That responsibility lies in the hands of the young people who participate. The group projects become *their* successes or failures. The adults serve as facilitators. For example, if one of the young people is in charge of publicity, the adult youth leader might show the student how to do the job. Once he understands how to do it, it becomes his responsibility. The process looks something like this:

> I do it—they watch
> I do it—they help
> They do it—I help
> They do it—I watch

ALLOW YOUNG PEOPLE TO FAIL

Caution: Don't do anything for the youth in your group that they are capable of doing for themselves. Violate this principle at the risk of creating a group of spiritual babies who rely on adult leaders instead of learning to trust God.

Jesus emphasized this principle many times. When Peter asked if he could join Jesus in His walk on the water (Matthew 14:29), Jesus encouraged him to jump right in! We don't know exactly what happened next. Maybe Andrew yelled, "Watch out for the wave on the right, Pete!" But for some reason, Peter took his eyes off Jesus, got scared, and began to sink. Jesus allowed Peter to learn through failure. Through his failure he learned to keep his eyes on the Lord.

In the parable of the prodigal son (Luke 15), the father allowed his son to fail. The father knew the boy would waste his money in riotous living, but he also knew that some things can only be learned through failure. When the son came to his senses, the father was waiting with open arms.

It is an alarming fact that students who were once committed members of high school youth groups "drop out" of church life at a staggering rate when they reach the college years. One reason for this high dropout rate is that we treat high schoolers as if they were still in diapers. We don't challenge them to think. Instead, we encourage them to regurgitate the words we give them without thinking the ideas through.

Then they hit the university campus. Some atheistic professor asks, "Who believes in the Bible?" Our little Alberta raises her hand. Then the prof asks, "Why?" Alberta responds with an answer that says in effect, "Because my adult youth group leader said I should." The professor proceeds to slice little Alberta into a hundred pieces and have her for lunch. She never knows what hit her.

We need to teach our young people that life is not a game with cheerleaders yelling, "Go, Christian, go!" Instead, it's a battlefield. Better that young people fail in the youth group and succeed in the world than vice versa.

This is not always an easy principle to practice, as I discovered when I met for a year with a group of eight high-school-age student leaders. Every Wednesday night for a year, we would meet to study the Gospel of John. I would give the eight students the lesson material on Wednesday. The following Monday night, in pairs, they would give the same material to their peers in four different homes.

On Wednesday nights, after forty-five minutes of my ramblings on the passage in John, I would ask the students if they were ready to present the lesson. They would all nod affirmatively. Then I would fire a difficult question at them about the passage. They would moan and complain: "No one will think of asking that," or "How are we supposed to know?" or "That's too hard." Then we would begin searching for the answer in commentaries, concordances, word study books, and Bible atlases. When the students could answer the question satisfactorily, I would ask them another. This process would go on for another forty-five minutes.

The kids would get so mad at me I could see it in their eyes. I would tangle and dangle them till they wondered whose side I was on. *But*—when they left that room they left with eyes of steel, muttering under their breath to the world, "Ask me a question from this passage in John! Ask me anything!"

When students such as these hit the university campus, they *look* for the atheistic profs and sit in the front row with their oversized Bibles prominently displayed. They can hardly wait for the prof to challenge their faith.

What makes the difference? Allowing young people to fail. We must allow them to fail, to fall flat on their posteriors if need be. We overreact to pressure in a teen's life, especially if it's causing pain and we think we can do something to relieve it. Instead of helping them work through it, we think of how we can get them out of it.

Becky was responsible for publicity in our youth group. We had an important activity coming up that we hoped would attract a lot of non-Christian kids. But Becky only completed half of the publicity and left it unfinished with a note on my desk. She was hoping I would finish it for her.

I called her home and explained that the publicity was Becky's responsibility and that if she didn't do it, it wouldn't get done. Becky didn't complete it and only half the number of kids we were expecting showed up.

The following Monday, Becky came into my office. I asked her what happened. She explained and said that she felt she had let down the whole group. I agreed with her and asked what she thought she should do next.

"Maybe I should just quit!" she responded.

"Quit? Quit!" I replied.

"Well, maybe I shouldn't quit," said Becky.

We talked about responsibility and commitment. Becky saw how she could change her priorities and schedule in order to get things done. We prayed together that God would use her. Becky was a dynamite publicity chairwoman from that day on. I could always count on her.

Becky is now married and is an active leader of a large "young married" group at our church. Becky learned by being allowed to fail—and then dust herself off and go at it again.

OTHER RESPONSIBILITIES AND OPPORTUNITIES

The most important responsibility of every youth volunteer is to be there—at every meeting and at every special event. The first task of a youth worker, after all, is to build relationships—and that takes time. You can't afford to miss any opportunity. You must be there for everything—not simply as a chaperone, but as an active participant in the lives of young people.[1]

Another responsibility of the adult volunteer is to visibly and audibly support the youth program—to identify his goals with the group's goals and to act as a bridge of communication to members in the church who may misunderstand what the group is doing.

Each youth worker will have his own style of ministry. There is no absolute guideline as to how authoritative to be in a youth group. But remember—and remind your volunteers—that youth are more likely to participate willingly and cheerfully when they have a part in the decision making. Maybe you're the kind of leader who makes the decisions and tells the group what to do. Maybe you like to make the decision and then try to sell it to the group. Or maybe you're the type of leader who asks for opinions from the young people and then makes the decision in the light of those opinions. I prefer leaders who go one step further than that—who present the issue to the group and then work through the issue *with* the youth group, eventually arriving at a solution or answer together.[2]

There are two ways to do youth activities. One is to be adult centered—the adult does everything and the kids come to be entertained. The other is kid centered—the kids do everything (reserve facilities, give Bible Study, opening prayer, lead singing, plan games, clean up, and so on). There are lots of advantages to the second method: When the youth are responsible, they're far less critical of the program. They have a sense of ownership, a sense of pride in their group. And letting the kids take responsibility for much of the legwork frees the adult volunteer to be a facilitator, enabler, and encourager. Of course, there are some things young people can't do. It wouldn't be real wise to let a junior higher drive the church bus to camp. Also, during the Sunday school hour, the adult volunteer may want to take the bulk of the teaching time, but still involve the young people in discussions, activities, and skits.

If your youth group has a weekly youth meeting, the adult volunteer team may want to divide the responsibilities (such as singing, group prayer time, crowdbreaker games, brief devotion or Bible Study, refreshments, and clean up) among themselves. Then, for variety and fairness, each month they should rotate those responsibilities.

As I stated earlier, the adults in charge of each of these areas don't necessarily do them alone. It's best for them to recruit young people from the group and work with them during the week before the meeting. Then when meeting day comes, the kids are responsible for their portion of the evening and the adult volunteers sit with the rest of the kids, silently praying for the young people up front.

7.
EQUIPPING AND
TRAINING VOLUNTEERS

Volunteers need training. Most feel totally inadequate. They're afraid you'll dump them into a roomful of young people and leave them there. They need to be assured that you won't desert or ignore them. That's why your training program shouldn't be a mystery to anybody—including yourself. Every volunteer who signs on should know what kind of training you provide, and when.

But there is training and there is training. Just as you have chosen your volunteers for the diversity of their talents and qualifications, so their training needs differ also. And the types of training events you'll plan will vary with the results you hope to accomplish. For instance, some of your training events will be for the purpose of recruiting—and weeding out—prospective volunteers. Others will be for the purpose of continuing, on-the-job training for volunteers already active in your youth program.

A STRATEGY FOR AN INITIAL TRAINING
EVENT FOR PROSPECTIVE VOLUNTEERS

Some adults, despite their best intentions, do not cope well with young people. Adolescents are viewed as problems to be solved, not as people to be loved. Communication grinds to a halt while one misunderstanding after another builds a wall between youth and adult. Not everyone has the temperament to work with young people. For these people, youth work just does not work out.

David O. Moberg in *The Church as a Social Institution* points out:

> Volunteers for teaching assignments and other youth leadership positions often include those least capable to take such responsibility. Many inner needs of such persons are met by religious service. Among them release of guilt, relief from boredom, and escape from family tension. Volunteers are sometimes selfishly grasping for solutions to their own problems, subconsciously subordinating the church's welfare to their own personal needs.[1]

As discussed elsewhere in this book, the best way to attract qualified volunteers and weed out those who are just not suited for youth work is to offer an initial, introductory training event for prospective volunteers—no commitment required, exploratory only. Spending that time with those new prospects should give you a reasonable feel for which ones will work well with your youth and which will not.

Some of the following ideas were suggested by David Roadcup in *Recruiting, Training, and Developing Volunteer Youth Workers.*[2]

Time of Seminar

Select a weekend in which you can expect the greatest amount of participation from your anticipated workers.

The basic initial training could be offered quarterly, semiannually, or yearly. You can, if you want, invite existing volunteers and use this as a refresher course for them, as well as an introductory course for those just starting or considering working with young people.

The training could be offered in the Sunday morning Sunday school as a four-week series. Another possibility is to conduct it on a Saturday morning or afternoon. Or try conducting the seminar two evenings a week for two weeks, working two hours each session. Be sure to divide the two-hour session into two parts, however, or the two hours will seem very long; here's one possible schedule:

7:30–8:30: Part I
8:30–8:45: Refreshment Break
8:45–9:30: Part II

For those who want to be part of your staff but can't attend the sessions, tape each session and allow them to listen on their own time and bring their questions to you later.

Here's another scheme: have an introductory "tea" with potential workers, followed by a self-paced, taped training program to be completed by the potential worker within a two-week period. You may then want to give them a little test at the end of it.[3]

Location

Your church building will probably be the best place to meet—you'll have audiovisual equipment, meeting rooms, and babysitting facilities. For less formal meetings, you may want to choose a large home.

Preparation

Be sure to have your lectures, discussion starters and discussion questions, and visuals (overhead transparencies, charts, and others) thoroughly planned and prepared in advance.

Choose a room that *enhances* your presentations, rather than detracts from them. Meeting in an auditorium that seats 700 with 45 people present wouldn't exactly promote good group dynamics. Make sure the room fits the number of people present. And make sure it's well ventilated. The temperature should be comfortable. Check well in advance to make sure the room is heated or cooled properly and that the lighting is adequate.

Notebook

Issue to each worker (not one per couple) a *Worker's Resource Notebook*—a three-ring binder into which they can put the outlines of the presentations you or your resource people will provide. Be sure and allow space for note-taking on the outlines themselves, and make sure the outline pages are three-hole punched. Provide pencils. These notebooks are an expense the church budget will have to cover, of course, but providing them makes it much more likely that your prospective volunteers will keep and possibly review the seminar material.

Resource Table

Displaying available resources during the seminar is an excellent idea. You can display all of the materials owned by the church, those in your personal library, and possibly materials loaned from a local library or Christian bookstore. This will allow your sponsors to begin to become familiar with materials at their disposal. You might even make arrangements to sell materials obtained from a bookstore at the seminar.

Additional Tips

1. It is important to provide babysitting for the children of the potential workers. Some may not come if you don't.

2. Refreshments for breaks should be provided at no cost.

3. If your training event occurs during lunch or breakfast, the church should provide the meal—if not, arrange for everyone to participate in a "potluck" meal.

4. All who attended your initial training session should be given an individual personal interview within a few days afterward to discuss if and where they would be best suited in youth ministry.

5. There is a lot of discussion over the length of

commitment desirable in a volunteer. I am looking for lifers—volunteers who want to have some roots in this ministry. You may feel more comfortable having a one-year commitment to be reviewed each year. The only problem I have with this is that you may be stuck with someone you don't want for a year (365 days, 8,760 hours, or 525,600 minutes)—and the volunteer, who may not care for the ministry either, may feel trapped. I have an open-ended commitment. My volunteers can get out anytime. Of course, I hope they won't come up to me on Sunday and say, "So long, it's all yours"; I hope they'll be sensitive and give me a couple of month's notice before they leave. The team ministry concept also allows for this. When there are three or four working with one age group, the others can carry the load for awhile if one leaves.

6. In planning a training seminar, if you anticipate a small group you may want to consider combining forces with another church. If you don't feel adequate to do the training, you might consider bringing in a specialist. This may be a wise move even if you *do* feel adequate, because someone else can say the same thing you have been saying for years and suddenly it hits home with your people.

ADVANCED TRAINING

Most of the training your volunteers will receive will be on-the-job training—hands-on experience being with the young people. Some things simply cannot be taught in the classroom setting and must be experienced in the arena of life. But they'll need more than that—they'll need seminars, workshops, discussions—actual training events that deal specifically with the areas of youth work they're responsible for.

But be careful: There is a tendency in recruiting volunteers to rush into an intensive training program. You may scare them off by overwhelming them with so much information. They may also not be ready or see the need for what you are giving them in a training seminar—especially if you've been too quick with the "hows" before establishing the "whys." We tend to explain "how" to be a youth worker without letting them see "why" they need the training session.

I ran head on into this principle several years ago. I had a group of high schoolers who wanted to share their faith and be more evangelistic. I was thrilled! So, I got them together one Saturday to teach a two-hour seminar on how to share your faith. They were bored silly. They kept moving around in their chairs and counting the holes in the ceiling. Fifteen minutes into my lecture on "How to Share Your Faith," it dawned on me that I had not established *why* they needed these lessons. So I stopped—and sent them to a local park in our city to talk to people cold turkey about Jesus.

They dragged into my office an hour later. They were dying. People had asked them questions they had no answers for; they couldn't remember particular verses; they were tongue-tied. They were practically gasping as they asked me to teach them how to share their faith. This time they were on the edge of their seats—listening to exactly the same material. What made the difference? The difference was that I had established the "whys."

As I speak around the country, it's easy for me to tell which youth workers have been working with the troops for awhile and which are at the workshop because they are *thinking* about going into youth work. Those just considering youth ministry are sitting back in their chairs with looks of, "I'm sure this is helpful for some, but it seems pretty basic and simple to me." Those that have been out in the field, those who have already learned the *whys* for this workshop, are on the edge of their seats with looks that say, "Help me, anything you've got I want—just help."

So, before you jump into an advanced training seminar, make sure you're not trying to cover everything they need to know in one shot. Also, make sure that you've established the reasons they need to be in that seminar.

Advanced training could be a one-day shot or an entire weekend retreat. If you decide to do a retreat, schedule a minimum of thirty-six hours together (one night and all the next day). The retreat will offer time at a site away from the church and interruptions. This could not only be a time of training and learning, but also a time to deepen friendships and offer opportunities to form new friendships, as well as a time of personal spiritual growth away from the kids. They will come back from the retreat rested, relaxed, inspired and confident about their role in the program. [4]

Encourage your workers to leave their children with grandparents or friends for this overnight stay. It is also wise to take people from the church (perhaps parents of young people in your program who are not volunteer workers) to do the cooking, if you go to a location where you must provide your own meals. Staff workers who also must prepare the food or look after children will miss much of the content of the retreat.

A retreat is an excellent time to bring in a special resource person to do the information sessions. If you do, be sure you've thoroughly discussed with that speaker the topics to be covered, the retreat schedule, and any other pertinent information.

Below is a suggested retreat schedule: [5]

Friday

7:30: Arrive at facility and get settled in
8:00: Warm up, body life, or small groups
8:30: Information session I
9:30: Breakout/discussion groups
10:30: Snacks
10:30: Campfire, sharing, and praise

Saturday

8:00: Breakfast
9:00: Small groups

123

  9:45: Information session II
10:45: Coffee break
11:00: Information session III
12:00: Lunch
  1:00: Volleyball or other recreation
  2:00: Feedback and discussion session
  3:00: Commitment service
  3:30: Home

SIX STEPS TO A COMPLETE TRAINING PROGRAM

In *The Youth Leaders Source Book,* Mike West has established a step-by-step process to organize a training program for volunteers.[6]

1. Identify the task to be completed. Determine at the beginning of your ministry what your goals and needs are. Goal-oriented people know where they are going with the young people God has entrusted to them. Clearly defined goals put handles on your dreams. Goals are important. If your youth group has no goals it will:

- cover too much ground
- major in the minors
- have a tendency to ramble
- not be related to life needs
- have few or no results

Goals are important—without them, it's hard to figure out what ought to be happening from one meeting to the next. Goals are also motivators. They help us get going each day. Goals give youth groups purpose and direction. They bring the future into the present. They help us realize our dreams.

The long-range goals stated in chapter 6 are to bring young people to maturity in Christ (Colossians 1:28) and prepare them for some form of ministry (Ephesians 4:12). The short-range goals you establish for your youth group will be based on their needs and will differ from year to year. These goals need to be attainable, yet challenging; they need to be measurable, realistic, and accomplishable.

The first step in planning your training strategy, then is to list specific goals you want to see achieved, tasks you want to see accomplished. This will help determine the needs your training program will address.

2. Identify the skills and knowledge needed to accomplish each task. After you've listed the youth group's needs and the tasks those needs require, divide the list into workable units, listing the skills necessary to complete them. For example: If one of the tasks is to have a winter retreat, the skills required for that task would be to organize, schedule, coordinate, recruit, motivate, and run meetings. The type of knowledge needed would be familiarity with the needs of the group, possible locations, potential resources, budget restrictions, and awareness of what has happened in the past with the winter retreat.

3. Prioritize tasks according to overall impact. There are certain tasks that are necessary for the spiritual health of your group. Such things as the development of student leadership, small group Bible studies, personal appointments, and well-run retreats are almost indispensable items to a healthy youth group.

There are other tasks that establish a "tone" for your ministry. They could include the quality of group singing, the enthusiasm of the opening sessions in Sunday school, and the general appearance of your meeting area. Whatever you see as important must be given a high priority.

4. Match people with tasks. This is a crucial step. In the process of selecting your volunteer staff, you will have obtained a clear idea of what their gifts are. Your training program should place people in positions that allow them to exercise those gifts while accomplishing the task that you have identified as important to your group. By placing people where they belong, you will also be cutting down on turnover. When people are using their strengths and contributing to the success of your program, their motivation for staying will be increased greatly, their commitment to the group sealed, and the quality of ministry increased.

5. Determine training needs of volunteers based on the task they will be performing. After you have assigned a task to a person, ask yourself: "What can training do to help this person do that task?" If a person has the task of leading the singing and is an expert in that field, training may not be important for the *performance* of that task—but it may be necessary to help that individual apply his skills to a youth ministry context or to help integrate his contribution with those of the rest of the staff. Training should solve problems, answer questions, and meet the needs of your volunteers, at a variety of levels.

6. Develop a training curriculum that imparts the right kind of knowledge, teaches the needed skills, and builds a positive attitude. Such a curriculum can be divided into three different categories. First, volunteers need input that teaches them the "how tos" of ministry:

- Using the media in youth ministry
- Leading small groups
- Building personal relationships
- Leading students to Christ
- Discipling young people
- Giving a talk
- Leading discussions
- Motivating youth
- Using audio/visuals
- Discipline
- Publicity
- Mission and service
- Creativity
- Counseling
- Working with parents
- Fun and games (recreation)

As you help your staff develop these skills, they will increase not only their efficiency but also their sense of satisfaction on mastering a ministry skill that they will be able to use in other situations.

A second level of instruction should deal with the reasons behind the "how tos." Because volunteers are usually involved in tasks that represent just a *piece* of the "ministry pie," it is easy for volunteers to lose their perspective, to fail to see how all the rest of the pieces of the pie fit in. Expose volunteers to ideas that deal with:

- Importance of youth ministry
- Philosophy of youth ministry
- Youth characteristics
- Youth culture
- Job descriptions

As volunteers are exposed to these and other materials that touch on the reasons behind their activities, they'll be better able to see how their own task fits into the whole. For example, if one of your volunteers is doing a Bible study for a group of typical high school sophomores, he could be discouraged if he interpreted "sophomore indifference" as a comment on the quality of his class or of the kids' opinion of him. If he understands that indifference is a normal part of adolescent behavior, and if he understands the discipleship process, he'll be better able to persist in his ministry, anticipating what can happen as the kids mature emotionally, physically, socially, and spiritually.

A third area that your training program should deal with is the *personal* needs of your staff.

- Characteristics of an effective youth worker
- Time management
- Prayer and meditation
- Getting into the Bible
- Family
- Self-image

SUPERVISION OF VOLUNTEERS

Because ministry does not take place in the classroom, a responsible training program follows through to the supervision of volunteers as they do their tasks. Supervision is a structured way of relating to people. It is a consistent extension of a philosophy of training that cares for both people and programs. Proper supervision tells the volunteers they are important and that what they are doing is important.

As a supervisor you will encourage people in their tasks, monitor the progress of their ministry, serve as a catalyst for their abilities, and stimulate new learning.

Supervision requires consistent contact with a specific purpose: the personal edification of the volunteer and the enhancement of the kingdom of God. Supervision is a cooperative effort in which the relationship between people involved is the most important part of the learning experience. And that relationship should not be forced by an organizational chart. Instead, it is discipleship. It is a relationship involving trust, a common spirit of commitment, a mutual desire to learn, a willingness to pursue truth, and a belief that God will bless the faithfulness of that relationship.

PROVIDING ADEQUATE RESOURCES AND TOOLS

Let volunteers know what is available to them in the way of books, media, and money. Make sure they have the right tools for the job. Establish, if you can, a youth worker's library in an easy-to-get-at part of the church. Include books, magazines, articles on youth ministry philosophy, and those with practical, "how-to" ideas. Give them inspirational books to keep them going spiritually. Give them catalogs listing films and explain how they can order them. One of the most helpful resource tools is the *Resource Directory for Youth Workers* (Zondervan/Youth Specialties, 1986). It includes the names and addresses of some eight hundred publishers, organizations, distributors, books, films, agencies, periodicals, and people who might fill a need in your youth ministry.

Volunteers also need to know what money has been allocated for their use and how to get it. (One way of seeing how committed a church is to youth ministry is to check what portion of the church budget has been designated for youth work.) Give them money for meals and other expenses when they're required to be somewhere. Give them free tickets to concerts and events that they are required to attend with the kids. Babysitting money should be provided by the church for all volunteers at all youth events, including weekend youth retreats.

Let volunteers know what kind of rooms and facilities are available on the church property, as well as what others exist in the area (parks, retreat centers, community buildings, colleges, and so on).

Don't forget that other churches and organizations sponsor training events in your area. Check into denominational, district, and diocesan training. Take them to conventions, seminars, workshops, and clinics. Youth Specialties, Inc., has top-notch youth workers' seminars in more than fifty cities across the United States and Canada designed to meet the needs of both the veteran and rookie youth worker. The seminar will involve, encourage, equip, and renew the volunteer's enthusiasm for youth work. *Group* magazine also offers excellent seminars and workshops dealing with a variety of topics.

8.
KEEPING
VOLUNTEERS

It's no secret that youth sponsors don't usually serve very long. Of course, there are the obvious reasons for dropping out: The young married couple suddenly becomes a young family; the corporation transfers the sponsor; the adult sponsor discovers that he just isn't cut out for youth work.

What about those ex-sponsors whose families remain stable, who aren't transferred by the corporation, who love youth work—but leave anyway? They, too, have their reasons. This chapter will examine some of those reasons, and some of the things that you can do to prevent the loss of your volunteers. In general, there are three things you must do to keep your volunteers: support them personally, support them through your management style, and give them a vision for youth ministry.

PERSONAL SUPPORT

Hoards of youth sponsors leave youth work because they don't feel as if they have the support of the youth minister, the senior pastor, the church board, or the "shakers and movers" of the congregation. And sometimes, in truth, there *is* a coalition of some or all of these leaders either to actively "do in" a youth sponsor or to fail to support him.

You can't allow that to happen, much less allow yourself to take part in it. It is in everybody's best interests for you, as youth ministers or lay youth leaders, to support, encourage, and even defend your sponsors. Keep lines of communication open. When a problem comes up, deal with it with courage. Do not sacrifice sponsors for political ends.

In Philippians 2:25–30, the apostle Paul describes Epaphroditus not only as a fellow soldier but also as a friend. Likewise, in order to retain volunteers, we must be friends to them. Developing that friendship means spending time together apart from the church setting. Spending social time together. Going to lunches and dinners. Playing Monopoly, Risk, Uno, and Trivial Pursuit; going to ball games, movies; going on vacations together. Don't deceive yourself that, by simply working together with your volunteers, you'll get to know each other. You may well be so busy running around getting things done that you can work with a volunteer for three months before you find out that he lost his parents in a traffic accident a year ago. We *must* take the time to get to know each other.

Ridge Burns, now a youth minister in Southern California, was previously director of High School Ministries at Wheaton Bible Church in Wheaton, Illinois. He would spend every Tuesday night from 6:30 to 10:00 P.M. with his staff.

At one of his first meetings, he was sitting around one night talking about what they had eaten the night before. One couple had split a peanut butter and jelly sandwich between them; another guy had a TV dinner; another went out to McDonald's. They realized that none of them ate right because they were too busy. So they decided to have a potluck meal together before their Tuesday meeting; at least they would get one good meal a week! Eating together every week has changed that group. They have become relationship centered rather than task centered. There is no agenda. They just eat and talk. The next thing you know they are praying together or just caring for each other. One person will share about a kid who's struggling with his dad. Another leader will respond and they'll begin to discuss together how to tackle the problem. The agenda is set by the needs of the group, except for one meeting a month where Ridge sets aside a structured planning time. [1]

Those attempts to spend informal time developing friendships with your volunteers will result in some awkward moments, of course. When I first began as youth pastor of Eastside Christian Church, an adult volunteer, Al Van Beenen, invited me to go waterskiing with some of the high-school students. I'd never been skiing before. Al had me back his station wagon with his boat attached down the ramp into the water. He was sitting in the boat; I was in the driver's seat of the station wagon. He kept telling me to back up, but the boat wouldn't slide off the trailer—and the trailer began to jackknife. The water by this time was up to the bottom of the car door, but Al continued signaling me to back up. A few more feet—and the car stalled. The station wagon was floating! Then the water began to pour in, and I ended up swimming out the window. As I was swimming to shore, two coeds from my college who happened to be at the lake that day saw me and said, "Les, is that you?" I wanted to die!

We had to tow the car out. Al never could get rid of the smell and finally had to sell the wagon. But he worked with our youth department for fifteen years, and each year he would go with the college group waterskiing for a week at the California Delta.

Spending informal time with your volunteers makes it easier for you to transfer your vision of youth ministry. It also allows the volunteers to verbalize their feelings, attitudes, and impressions in a nonthreatening environment. Allow them to talk. If you must speak, ask questions or repeat the volunteer's earlier statements to prompt him to take those thoughts further: How do you feel about . . . , I sense that . . . , How do you see . . . , What I hear you saying is . . . , What would you like . . . , Looks like you are . . .

SUPPORT THROUGH MANAGEMENT

Each of us has his own, individual style of management. Some of us are more authoritative than others; some of us are long on organization, others on interpersonal relationships.

What's crucial to remember when we're working with volunteers is that the way we choose to supervise them will have a direct impact on how comfortable they are in working with our youth program—and on how long they stay with us. Here are some of the ways we can adapt our management style to keep our volunteers happy.

Keep Them Informed

"Work with people, not around them." Every youth worker should have that slogan on his desk. To consistently work around an organizational leader creates two problems. First, it's embarrassing to a volunteer leader for a young person in his area of ministry to get information before he does. He's constantly playing catch-up, like the scoutmaster who puffed to the top of the hill and asked the farmer, "Have you seen ten scouts pass this way? I'm their leader." A volunteer leader who is constantly bypassed without good reasons will soon ask whether he's the leader or not.[2]

The second pitfall of bypassing organizational leaders is the increased burden you'll have to shoulder for the success or failure of the program. If you continually do the volunteer's job for him, he'll begin to feel that his services aren't needed and feel little or no responsibility for the success of the program. Ideally, it should work the opposite way: As the volunteer progresses in his ministry, he takes on more and more responsibility and the staff leader can withdraw some of the support that was needed in the beginning. It is a real joy to see a person grow in his responsibility. Someone has said that a staff leader's responsibility is to try to "work himself out of a job."

Resist the temptation to jump in and solve problems yourself. Let your volunteers work out on their own the problems they encounter. Handling those problems yourself creates expectations in your volunteers: The *next* time a problem occurs, they'll automatically look to you to handle it. And your volunteers' morale may suffer if you solve their problems for them, too—obviously, you didn't trust them to be able to work it out on their own. What seems to be the quickest way to handle a situation may turn into a continuing responsibility.

Allow Them To Be Themselves

Maybe Carl Rogers said it best in *Learning to Feel, Feeling to Learn:*

> I have come to think that one of the most satisfying experiences I know and also one of the most growth-promoting experiences for the other person is just fully to appreciate this individual in the same way that I appreciate a sunset. People are just as wonderful as sunsets if I can just let them be. In fact, perhaps the reasons we can truly appreciate a sunset is that we cannot control it. When I look at a sunset as I did the other evening, I don't find myself saying, "Soften the orange a little on the right hand corner, and put on a bit more purple along the base, and use a little more pink in the cloud color." I don't do that. I don't try to control the sunset. I watch it with awe as it unfolds. I like myself best when I can experience my staff member, my son, my daughter, in this same way, appreciating the unfolding of a life. . . . A person who is loved appreciatively, not possessively, blooms, and develops his own unique self. The person who loves non-possessively is himself enriched.[3]

Be a Motivator

A good motivator, of course, uses a number of means to motivate his coworkers. Let's discuss two of the most useful and effective in motivating youth ministry volunteers: enthusiasm and anger.

Enthusiasm as a motivator. To become good at motivating volunteers, I have to work at motivating myself. There's nothing quite so compelling as the person who is excited about his ministry opportunity and wants others to share the joy of ministry.

So—how is the motivator motivated? Here are four suggestions:

1. Associate with successful, positive people. Distance yourself, if necessary, from pessimistic people who pull you down. Spend your time with people who inspire you, who stimulate your thinking and restore your vision, who stretch your capacity for dreaming.

2. Monitor carefully the ideas entering your mind. As the computer people say, "garbage in, garbage out." If it's true that you become what you think, and if you feed a constant stream of junk and trivia into your brain, you are unlikely to be the strong persuader you want to be. You may need to turn off the TV and read instead.

3. Take advantage of the wealth of information now available on inexpensive audio cassettes. The wonderful thing about tapes is that not only do we get the ideas of great people but, by listening to their voices, we have a chance to experience their personalities and catch their energy and enthusiasm. So rather than letting the radio's stream of nonsense occupy your driving hours, listen to tapes of inspiring, accomplished speakers. According to a study made at the University of Southern California, if you drive twelve thousand miles each year, in three years' time you can acquire the equivalent of two years of college lectures.

4. Attend classes and seminars. It's worth a few hundred miles of travel and a few hundred dollars to audit courses taught by bright instructors where you can associate with other highly motivated people.

Enthusiasm is contagious. A few years ago, I was flying from Los Angeles to Cincinnati by way of Dallas, Texas. After we had taken off, I noticed a dozen or more ladies scattered throughout the plane, all wearing red, white, and blue straw hats. One of them was sitting next to me. I thought the hats were a bit unusual, but I soon forgot them—till the lady next to me got up and walked to the front of the crowded plane.

She faced all of the passengers and said, "Ladies, are we ready?" Suddenly, these ladies began to sing, "I've got the Mary Kay enthusiasm down in my heart. . . ." I was amazed!

Then she said to everyone, "Put down your drinks." A gray-haired, distinguished, fifty-five-year-old businessman on the other side of me put down his drink. I cracked up! Then the Mary Kay leader got the whole plane clapping as the ladies sang this little song.

When she finally sat down, I was dumbfounded. But I began to think—*if this woman is that enthusiastic about Mary Kay Cosmetics, how much more enthusiastic should I be about working with God's people?*

The word *enthusiasm* literally means "God in us." As Christians we have God living in us. How can we not be enthusiastic? The book of Acts shows how enthusiastic those early Christians were. For example: "We cannot stop telling about the wonderful things we saw Jesus do and heard Him say" (Acts 4:20, The Living Bible). Now that's enthusiasm!

When Dwight D. Eisenhower was president of Columbia University, he called John Erskine "the greatest teacher Columbia ever had."[4] Erskine was one of the most versatile men of his era—educator, concert pianist, author of sixty books, head of the Julliard School of Music, popular and witty lecturer. Writing about that remarkable career, his wife Helen attributed it to his "defiant optimism." He was a good teacher, she said, because of "his own excitement for learning and his trust in the future." He would tell her often, "Let's tell our young people that the best books are yet to be written; the best paintings have not yet been painted; the best governments are yet to be formed; the best is yet to be done by them."[5]

"Great [corporate] leaders understand human behavior rather than the cybernetics of any functional specialty,"[6] says James Schorr, executive vice-president of Holiday Inns, Inc. Translated, what he is saying is that a proven motivator will make it to the top before a proven genius. When Andrew Carnegie hired Charles Schwab to administer his far-flung steel empire, Schwab became the first man in history to earn a million dollars a year while in someone else's employ.

Schwab was once asked what equipped him to earn $3,000 a day. Was it his knowledge of steel manufacturing? "Nonsense," snorted Schwab. "I have lots of men working for me who know more about steel than I do." Schwab was paid such a handsome amount largely because of his ability to inspire other people. "I consider my ability to arouse enthusiasm among the men the greatest asset I possess," he said, and any leader who can do that can go almost anywhere. [7]

Youth workers aren't like people in large corporations who are paid well but often feel that they aren't making any significant difference in the lives of others. Youth work offers people the opportunity to make a visible difference in the lives of young people. Now that's something to be enthusiastic about—and if you *do* get discouraged, rent the black-and-white video with James Stewart called, "It's A Wonderful Life" (1946, Hal Roach Studio) or the original "Goodbye Mr. Chips" (1939, MGM/UA). Sometimes we have no idea of the impact we have made on people's lives.

Anger as a motivator. Alan Loy McGinnis in his book *Bringing Out the Best in People* suggests using anger as a motivator. [8] Idealists might suppose that the only way to inspire people is to appeal to their benevolent instincts. Not always true. The best motivators usually appeal to the anger in people as well. Why? Because enormous energies reside deep within us and come to the surface when we get angry. Martin Luther said: "When I am angry I can write, pray, and preach well, for then my whole temperament is quickened, my understanding sharpened, and all mundane vexations and temptations gone." [9] A little righteous indignation seems to bring out the best in the national personality. The United States was born when fifty-six patriots got angry enough to sign the Declaration of Independence. We put a man on the moon because Sputnik made us mad at being number two in space.

This motivational principle is well illustrated by Lee

Iacocca's use of *The Wall Street Journal.* In 1979 the paper published a scorching editorial criticizing Chrysler's mismanagement and saying that the nearly bankrupt company should be allowed to "die with dignity."

Iacocca got lots of mileage out of that quote. Rather than allowing it to damage him, or ignoring it and hoping people would forget it, he turned it around and used it to arouse passionate sympathy for his company's cause. Here is an excerpt from one of his speeches:

> *The Wall Street Journal* advised me to let Chrysler Corporation "die with dignity." After all we were flat broke. Our plants were industrial museums. The Michigan State Fairgrounds were full of our unsold cars.
>
> I got mad. . . . My colleagues in Highland Park got mad. Tens of thousands of Chrysler people all across America got mad. Our labor unions, our suppliers, and our lenders all got mad. We got so mad, we banded together, we talked things over, and working together, we fixed what was wrong at Chrysler.
>
> We doubled our productivity. We rejuvenated our factories. We cut our costs. We started building the highest quality cars and trucks made in America. In short, we turned things around. Now, we're selling cars and making lots of money. . . . This story has a moral. Wonderful things can happen when Americans get mad. I think some well-directed anger can cure most of what's wrong in America today.[10]

Very few people listening to Iacocca's speech could keep from having a visceral reaction—a speech like this makes you want to support the underdog.

Is anger seen as a negative force in the Bible? The Hebrew words that are translated "anger" or "angry" in the Old Testament occur almost 455 times, and nearly 375 of these refer to God's anger. Christ blazed with anger at the scribes and Pharisees, and the Scriptures paint life in general as warfare: We wrestle against forces of evil, against principalities and powers of darkness.

Any powerful motivational speaker uses the entire panoply of emotions to stir the listener, and anger is certainly one of them. Mark Twain was fond of saying that to hold a crowd you must alternate between wooing them and abusing them; all good platform speakers, like good coaches, will occasionally display anger at their audiences. They will also arouse anger *in* their audiences, as Iacocca did in his famous speech about *The Wall Street Journal*.

Appealing to anger and the competitive spirit does another thing: it tends to pull people together. A large family may have lots of sibling squabbles at the dinner table, but if one of those children is criticized by someone from the outside and that fact is aired at the table, cohesiveness builds in a hurry. And a congregation that is fighting internally can quickly forget its intramural differences if it is inspired to take on some common enemy.

In fact, churches furnish us with interesting microcosms for watching how group morale is built and destroyed. For all our religious talk about love, I have never seen a congregation genuinely fired up unless that congregation was united in fighting some common enemy. The adversaries may be very different for different types of churches, but it seems essential to find something to oppose.

Remember, of course, that there can be—and often are—unscrupulous or unspiritual appeals to our anger. Propagandists can fan the flame of hatred to horrible ends. Wars and lynchings are also the result of group anger. Hitler aroused enormous energy and cohesiveness by using the Jews as scapegoats, and when Jim Jones convinced 912 people to commit suicide together, he did it by constructing a paranoid, illusionary world for his followers to hate. Both are illustrations of appeals to anger that have run amuck.

We can avoid such excesses if we appeal sparingly to people's competitive instincts and choose our enemies carefully. There is nothing wrong with godly anger aimed in the right direction: poverty, world hunger, prejudice, drugs, cruelty, and deceit. I am not endorsing cruel, hot-headed, uncontrolled rage directed at an individual. We must also refrain from creating straw men in order to pull people to our side. Our world contains plenty of abuses to oppose without having to create artificial ones.

Have High Expectations

When I was younger, I was always taught that if you have high expectations of people, you'll always be disappointed. Not necessarily true—in fact, it often works just the opposite. When others have high expectations of you, then there is more incentive to perform well. Warren Bennis, in *The Unconscious Conspiracy: Why Leaders Can't Lead*, finds ample reason to agree: "In a study of school teachers, it turned out that when they held high expectations of their students, that alone was enough to cause an increase of 25 points in the student's IQ scores."[11] It was Emerson who said, "Our chief want in life is someone who will make us do what we can."

One of the biographers of Ghandi said this about him, "He refused to see the bad in people. He often changed human beings by regarding them not as what they were but as though they were what they wished to be."[12] Our job is to give volunteers confidence that God is working in and through them. Remember these are ordinary people in the hands of an extraordinary God. We need to communicate to volunteers that they are someone in whom we have confidence. We need to be affirmers, encouragers, and cheerleaders for these volunteers. Sometimes all they need is a good locker room pep talk.

I'll never forget the first time I preached in a church service. I had become a Christian at age sixteen and had done a little street preaching on Sunset Strip in Hollywood, but I had never spoken in a church building to a Christian group. The Christian college I attended sent some of its students out to speak at neighborhood churches on Sunday evenings. The first time I went, I was extremely nervous. A girl from the college came with me to do special music.

There were fifteen or twenty people attending that night.

They started the service by singing a song I disliked, "Beulah Land." (I never could get into going to Beulah Land, and some of the words seemed so negative—"in God's Word retreating.") By the end of the song I was starting to perspire.

The girl from the college got up to sing her special music. She was nervous, too. She got her heel caught in an old metal floor heater in the center aisle and fell on her posterior, crushing not only her dress but her pride. She managed to get through her song, and then it was time for me to get up and preach.

I was scared to death. In the pew in front of me sat one little gray-haired man. I grabbed the back of the pew to get up, not realizing that it wasn't fastened down. The pew flipped over, dumping the man onto the floor. I picked him up and dusted him off, apologizing profusely, and made my way to the pulpit.

I had worked on four sermon outlines, and finally decided to go with my sermon about the apostle Peter. I talk fast, even when I'm calm. That evening, I went through my entire "Peter Sermon" in three-and-a-half minutes. In eleven minutes, I had clipped through all four of my sermon outlines. When I finished speaking, I wanted to crawl out of the building. I concluded that God could better use me as an assistant manager of a K-Mart store.

On the way out, a little old lady grabbed my arm. I was prepared for the worst. Looking me in the eye she said, "Son, that was tremendous! Why that was better than the apostle Paul would have done." Any idiot with half a brain cell functioning could have found forty things wrong with what I had done that night, but this little lady chose instead to be encouraging—so encouraging, in fact, that I walked out of the church saying to myself, "Billy Graham, move over. Here I come!"

Unfortunately, too many of us are more like the grandfather who fell asleep in his rocking chair. The grandson came in and put Limburger cheese on the grandfather's moustache. He soon awakened and said, "My, this room stinks." He walked around the house and said, "This whole house stinks." Then he walked outside and said, "This whole neighborhood stinks." Of course, it wasn't the neighborhood, or the house, or the room—it was him.

Sometimes we get so discouraged that we're ready to throw in the towel and say, "These volunteers stink." It may not be the volunteers—it may be us! We may need to wipe the Limburger cheese off and pray that God will help us view the situation more positively.

According to Acts 4:36, Barnabas' name means "son of encouragement." Volunteers need youth workers who will be Barnabases to them. This is a team ministry, and teams work best when they're made up of people who love and support each other. I saw this saying on a bulletin board: "Caretakers in a mental ward are not afraid of the patients. Crazy people never unite on anything." Volunteers need to be a part of a loving, caring community of believers.

A leader's job is to take two steps forward and then, if you don't step on a land mine, you turn to the troops and say, "Come on." They will do one of three things: (1) Follow you; (2) Sit down right where they are; or (3) Shoot you. Beware: The leader who gets too far ahead of the troops is soon mistaken for the enemy. Many times we fall into the trap of playing the role of the cowboy instead of the shepherd. A cowboy gets behind and drives the cattle with a whip. A shepherd goes in front, saying, "Follow me." Most of us tend toward the cowboy style of leadership because that's all we have ever known. Learn to be a shepherd instead.

Be Generous With Nonmonetary Rewards

Let volunteers know they are appreciated. Volunteers need to be affirmed, and we need to be aggressive affirmers—especially with nonmonetary incentives. *Leadership* ran this little article, written by a parishioner to his minister:

Here's what I mean, for example. Take Eddie Turner with his five kids, three of them teenagers. He's into everything. Practically eats and sleeps at the church. Now what if someone said to him, "Hey, Eddie, two kids in the youth group accepted the Lord this week. All that driving around you've done to take the kids to Camp Ocheewahbee and the roller rink and every place really helped. You had a part in it." Not that Eddie needs anyone to say thanks, you understand. But the way he's going, he's going to need a little encouragement.

Well, to close, pastor, like I said, I haven't dropped out. Maybe I just need to hear you say it once more: "Wilson, it's the ninth inning and we're two runs behind. We've got two outs and no one on and you're up. We're counting on you to hit, because Eddie Turner is right behind you and he's the best clutch hitter we've got and he leads in RBI's. So go get 'em." [13]

There are several other ways to convey this appreciation:

✓ **1.** Recognize your volunteers' contributions verbally in front of the young people, their peers, and the entire church.

✓ **2.** Give them a phone call—tell them how special you think they are and fill them in on how they have positively affected some kids' lives.

✓ **3.** Write them a personal note of thanks and appreciation. Share the positive comments you have heard about them.

✓ **4.** If they handle a sticky, delicate situation, let them know it. Have them share with the rest of the group how they handled the situation.

✓ **5.** Mention them in the church newsletter, Sunday morning bulletin, or local newspaper.

6. Ask the senior minister or chairman of the board to write your volunteers a letter expressing his appreciation.

7. David Stone recognizes adults who have made special contributions by having all the youth stand on cue and give them an "O'vation." All the young people stand with their arms over their heads in the shape of an "O" and say, "OOOOOOOOOOO!" [14]

8. Send the volunteer's spouse or family a note letting them know what a great job the volunteer has been doing and how you appreciate their willingness to allow this person to participate in the youth activities.

✓ **9.** Have a volunteer appreciation dinner—a banquet where you can recognize *all* the volunteers.

10. Take them on a retreat without the kids to get their spiritual batteries recharged.

11. Plan a worship service honoring all volunteers.

12. Send them birthday and anniversary cards.

Don't let volunteers feel used or unappreciated. Everybody needs a few strokes and a pat on the back, especially volunteers. Give them words of personal encouragement—especially immediately after they've done something noteworthy.

The Foxboro Corporation, in its early days, desperately needed a technical advance if the company was to survive. Late one evening, a scientist rushed into the president's office with a working prototype. Dumbfounded at the elegance of the solution and puzzled about how to reward it, the president rummaged through most of the drawers in his desk, found something, leaned over the desk to the scientist, and said, "Here!"

In his hand was a banana, the only reward he could immediately put his hands on. From that point on, the small "gold banana" pin has been the high accolade for scientific achievement at Foxboro.[15]

High-morale organizations have fun together. Too often the parent or the manager is guilty of growling, "Okay, we've had enough fun—let's get back to work," when the best work could be done while having fun. Thomas A. Edison once received a letter from a solemn stockholder. "A vice-president of your company," he wrote, "doesn't have a proper sense of dignity of his position and of his association with you. I'm told sometimes his laugh can be heard through his door and all over the office."

Edison sent the letter to the vice-president, tied to the framed picture of a laughing, jolly friar. "Hang this picture in the entrance hall," he wrote. "Have everyone around the office look at it. Let it be a constant reminder that good business is never done except in a reasonably good-humored frame of mind."[16]

Alan McGinnis, author of the bestseller *Bringing out the Best in People,* was interviewed once by a committee that laughed more frequently than any group of people he had ever seen. They had been meeting at least once a week for long sessions, and, though they were very different individuals, they worked together with a minimum of friction and with great enthusiasm. The secret, he thought, was in their laughter. The chairman, Harry Griffin, had structured the group that way from its inception. His philosophy was: "We're going to be together for hundreds of hours before this job is done. If we choose, we can grit our teeth and try to get it over with as soon as possible, with no monkey business allowed. Or we can decide to have some fun every time we meet. I vote for having fun." That did not mean that they wasted time but that in their meetings they always laughed. There was lots of affectionate ribbing of one another, and the result was a wonderful esprit de corps, which in turn enabled them to finish their task months sooner than expected.[17]

People never get to laugh as much as they'd like or have as much fun as they want, so if you can construct your class, your team, or your committee so that laughter breaks out frequently, you'll have people clamoring to join your group.

If there is a complaint volunteers most often express, it is this: "I never get any feedback from the boss—except when something goes wrong." And the teenagers who sit in my office tell me again and again, "My dad gets all over my case when I mess up at school, but when I bring home a good grade he acts as if it's nothing—that I'm finally doing what I should have been doing all along."

In *The One Minute Manager*, Blanchard and Johnson

suggest taking frequent breaks for what they describe as "One Minute Praisings." Catch your subordinate "doing something right," they advise, then give an immediate compliment. Seems easy enough, doesn't it? And we all know that such uncomplicated, straightforward praise is an effective way of reinforcing good work. But stop and think: How long has it been since you took a full sixty seconds to talk to your son or daughter about some fine thing they've just done? Or your secretary, or the volunteer who works with you?

Taking the time to thank people who help us is a basic courtesy that should apply in all human relations.

Be specific in your praise. Vague slaps on the back, like telling people that they're "doing a good job," don't have nearly the impact of a detailed commendation. "I liked the way you used the colors for the tree in your picture" registers with a five-year-old more than your saying, "That's a pretty picture." It shows that you have looked at it with care. Moreover, you are reinforcing specific behavior. Let's say that the big youth activity your volunteer staff planned was a smash hit with the kids. The volunteers may not be aware of the exact reasons they succeeded this time and failed at another time, so it's important for you to point out exactly what you liked and to show that you noticed how they worked overtime above and beyond what was agreed to in order to pull it off.

But remember this: Regular reinforcement loses impact because it comes to be expected. So unpredictable and intermittent reinforcement works best. Also, small rewards work better than large ones. Large rewards can discourage other volunteers who think they deserved them and can cause jealousy, bitterness, and hurt feelings.

Allow Them To Fail

Fear of failure can cripple a support team. You'll never develop competent volunteers unless you allow them room to fail without criticism. That fear of your criticism can make a volunteer afraid to try *anything* lest he fail. As William James said, "The art of being wise is to know what to overlook."[18] Every great leader has behind him a mental drawer full of failures that were good learning experiences and became building blocks to success.

Unfortunately, many leaders take a different tack and quickly find themselves frozen into the role of police officers. They think it's their duty to look over people's shoulders, to watch for errors, to discourage cheating—and to prevent failure. By adopting such a watchdog role, they quickly set up an adversarial relationship, and people will follow such bosses with all the relish of going in for a root canal. Good youth workers, on the other hand, don't waste much time doing postmortems on the failures of their volunteers. Instead they look for strengths that others have overlooked and for ways to encourage their volunteers' special gifts.

Encourage your volunteers to let their imaginations fly, to try new ideas, to take risks—even though by doing so they'll experience their share of failures, too. Encourage practical risk taking. Some churches *say* they encourage risk taking, but then punish even tiny failures. They want innovation, but kill the spirit of the volunteer. Emerson Corporation's president, Charles Knight, argues: "You need the ability to fail. You cannot innovate unless you are willing to accept mistakes."[19]

Diversified Christian leaders such as Swindoll, Falwell, Dobson, and Schuller have a common denominator: They all have a bushelful of failures—failures that resulted from risk taking.

Heinz's highly successful frozen foods subsidiary, Ore-Ida, is trying an intriguing variation of this theme in order to encourage more learning and risk taking in its research activities. It has carefully defined what it calls the "perfect failure," and shoots off a cannon in celebration every time one occurs. Here's their concept: All research and development is inherently risky, and the only way to succeed at all is through lots of tries; therefore, management's primary objective is to induce lots of tries, and a good try that results in some learning is to be celebrated even when it fails.[20]

I can think of many of my own failures in youth ministry, but one stands out. Fortunately for me, I had a boss who allowed me to fail and continue as youth minister. The details of the disaster were printed in *Youth Worker* under the title, "There's Power in the Blood":

> At one time I was a part-time youth minister in Garden Grove, California. When I first arrived at the church, the high school Sunday school room was painted hospital white. I suggested to the kids that we paint the room. They were excited about the project.
>
> It's usually difficult to get kids to do anything on a Saturday morning—especially work—but it wasn't at all difficult to get them to paint the room at the forbidden hour of 3:00 in the morning. We had a huge crowd. The problem was, we couldn't make up our minds what color to paint the room. Eventually, we decided to paint each wall a different color; bright red, bright blue, black and white. We then cleaned up and went out to breakfast.
>
> I forgot to mention two things: I didn't bother to ask anyone's permission to paint the room, and I neglected to ask the senior citizens (who shared the room with the youth) what they thought about the idea. I found out the next day. During the senior citizen's Sunday school hour, which met one hour before ours, they were talking about one thing—and it wasn't found in God's word.
>
> My senior minister suggested I could kiss my job good-bye if I didn't think of something fast! I decided to talk it over with the senior citizens at the end of their Sunday school class. I entered the room. Before they could say a word, I asked them if they had noticed that their room had been painted. They had. I then told them how excited I was to be working in a church where the high schoolers were so spiritual.
>
> I explained that the wall to their left was blue, to symbolize heaven; the wall to their right was red, to stand for the blood of Christ; the wall behind them was black, which stood for sin (they were facing away from that wall); and the front wall was white, for purity.

The church kept those colors in that room for eleven years. I mean, who could paint over the blood of Christ?[21]

Howard Head is a risk-taking champion par excellence. James Brian Quinn says of him and his revolutionary ski: "He was possessed by his idea, a fanatic on the subject."[22] To understand what champions are really like, read *Sports Illustrated's* story of Head's invention of the metal ski:

In 1946 Head went off to Stowe, Vermont, for his first attempt at skiing. "I was so humiliated and disgusted by how badly I skied," he recalls, "and, characteristically, I was inclined to blame it on the equipment, those long, clumsy hickory skis. On my way home I heard myself boasting to an Army officer beside me that I could make a better ski out of aircraft materials than could be made from wood.

Back at Martin, the cryptic doodles that began appearing on Head's drawing board inspired him to scavenge some aluminum from the plant scrap pile. In his off-hours he set up shop on the second floor of a converted stable in an alley near his one-room basement flat. His idea was to make a "metal sandwich" ski consisting of two layers of aluminum with plywood sidewalls and a center filling of honeycombed plastic.

Needing pressure and heat to fuse the materials together, Head concocted a process that would have made Rube Goldberg proud. To achieve the necessary pressure of 15 pounds per square inch, he put the ski mold into a huge rubber bag and then pumped the air out through a tube attached to an old refrigerator compressor that was hooked up backward to produce suction. For heat, he welded together an iron, coffinlike tank, filled it with motor oil drained from automobile crankcases and, using two Sears-Roebuck camp burners, cooked up a smelly 350-degree brew. Then he dumped the rubber bag with the ski mold inside into the tank of boiling oil and sat back like Julia Child waiting for her potato puffs to brown.

Six weeks later, out of the stench and smoke, Head produced his first six pairs of skis and raced off to Stowe to have them tested by the pros. To gauge the ski's camber, an instructor stuck the end of one into the snow and flexed it. It broke. So, eventually, did all six pairs. "Each time one of them broke," says Head, "something inside of me snapped with it."

Instead of hanging up his rubber bag, Head quit Martin the day after New Year's 1948, took $6,000 in poker winnings he had stashed under his bed, and went to work in earnest. Each week he would send a new and improved pair of skis to Neil Robinson, a ski instructor in Bromley, Vermont, for testing, and each week Robinson would send them back broken. "If I had known then that it would take 40 versions before the ski was any good, I might have given it up," says Head. "But fortunately, you get trapped into thinking the next design will be it."

Head wrestled with his obsession through three agonizing winters. The refinements were several: Steel edges for necessary bite, a plywood core for added strength, and a plastic running surface for smoother, ice-free runs. One crisp day in 1950, Head stood in the bowl of Tuckerman's Ravine in New Hampshire and watched ski instructor Clif Taylor come skimming into a long, graceful curve, swooshing to a stop in front of the beaming inventor.

"They're great, Mr. Head, just great," Taylor exclaimed. At that moment, Head says, "I knew deep inside I had it.[23]

Thomas Edison, at the height of his career, was producing one new patent every eight days. When he and his lab partners were working on the incandescent light bulb, they ran hundreds and hundreds of experiments and every one of them ended in failure. One day he walked into the lab and his partners gathered around him and said, "Tom, why don't we give up this stupid project. Nothing works. We have failed. Let's quit." Edison looked at those lab partners and said, "We have not failed once. We now know hundreds of things that didn't work. We are just that much closer to the solution." Within a matter of days they produced a workable light bulb. If he had listened to people who looked at failure negatively, he would have given up. He would have walked away when he was so close to success.

It was Seneca who said, "If thou art a man, admire those who attempt great things, even though they fail."[24] Theodore Roosevelt said, "The only man who never makes a mistake is the man who never does anything."[25] We should probably reprimand our staff if they are *not* having a few flops—if they're not failing now and then, it's a sign they're playing it safe.

I'm not saying that we should ignore failure. We must hold people accountable. But don't shoot someone or stab them in the back when all they need is a kick in the pants.

When You Feel Like A Failure

Have you ever felt like a failure, a reject? Ever get so discouraged you felt like even God couldn't believe what a turkey you've been? If you haven't yet, get ready—everyone in youth work has felt this at one time or another, especially as we're dealing with failure in others, such as volunteers or kids in the group. Often, in attempting to motivate others, I end up hitting the bottom of the barrel. We don't have an inexhaustible supply of spiritual power or mental capability. Every time we give, something goes out of us—the tank goes down. You can't interact with people at the transition points of their lives without arriving a little drained yourself, regardless of how popular you are or how well you get along with people or how good your song is.

Our work is difficult because we constantly deal with different people's expectations of us—from parents to the senior minister to the church board to the kids to other youth volunteers. Our work is also difficult because we never really finish it. Unlike a lawyer that ends a case, a carpenter that completes a table, an engineer that admires a completed bridge, or an architect that looks at a finished house, our work continues. Sisyphus, in Greek mythology, had the fate of pushing a great stone up a mountain only to have it roll down just before reaching the top. Many times we have that same feeling that our job is endless. We go home many times pounding the steering wheels of our cars feeling like failures.

As Howard Hendricks says:

> Failure is one of the uglies of life. We deny it, run away from it, or upon being overtaken, fall into permanent paralyzing fear. Probably because of our reluctance to face it, not much is

written about the anatomy of failure. As Christians, we wave
our visionary banners proclaiming "victory in Christ," refusing
often even to admit that the path to ultimate victory may
include intermediate bloody noses.[26]

There are many examples of failures in the Bible. In an
earlier chapter we mentioned Moses. There is also the
example of Mark (Acts 12), who deserted the missionary
venture of Paul and Barnabas. The best example to me is
that of Elijah.

What a contrast there is in the life of Elijah from I Kings
18 to I Kings 19. From the mountaintop to the valley, from
the thrill of victory to the agony of defeat, from his greatest
strength to his greatest weakness and failure. Jezebel was
infuriated with the news brought by King Ahab. After the
loss of her 450 prophets of Baal she was like a tigress robbed
of her young. She immediately put out a contract on Elijah's
life.

Elijah fled. Up until this time, the only thing that filled
Elijah's mind was Jehovah, but Elijah's whole world went
black with Jezebel's remark. She caught him when he was
emotionally exhausted. He was looking through the wrong
end of the telescope. The moment we take our eyes off the
sources of our courage, we lose it.

Elijah ran with bated breath and heaving chest, running
until his lungs would nearly burst. Running until his mouth
grew parched from inhaling the dry desert air. Running until
his powerful legs would carry him no longer in the scorching
desert heat. He collapsed under a broom bush and prayed
that he might die. Friends, he didn't want to die. It was a
foolish, hypocritical prayer. If he really wanted to die, I know
a woman 120 miles back who would have been glad to
accommodate him.

He was simply emotionally depressed and physically
fatigued. His tank was empty, his spiritual batteries were
dead. He felt beaten. He was ready to throw in the towel.
Isn't it ironic that single-handedly he takes on 450 prophets

of Baal, but one woman says, "I'm going to get you," and he runs! Elijah was overworked, overwrought, overworried, and over a barrel. He was in bad shape. There are some servants of God who will never get under a broom bush, but then they will never experience the heights of a Mount Carmel, either.

The verse that most intrigued me, that captured my attention, was I Kings 19:4 when Elijah says to God, "I am no better than my ancestors." The question I would have liked to ask Elijah was, "Who said you had to be?"

The favorite indoor sport of servants of God is to compare themselves with others. Always looking over their shoulders, comparing their ministries with someone else's. I start to compare myself with a Swindoll, Dobson, Campolo, or Graham, and I want to go home, get in a fetal position and suck my thumb! I'm crazy about them, but I'm not them.

I recently heard of a family who has a hobby of putting puzzles together as a family project. By now, they're pretty good at it, and they have to keep getting puzzles that are more and more difficult. One day the father brought home a new puzzle. But before he presented it to the family he switched the lid with another puzzle they hadn't put together in years. They worked for days, but gradually realized they couldn't put the puzzle together. The picture they were watching was not the same as the one they were working on. Only after they put the right picture with the right puzzle could they get it together.

It seems to me that this is what is happening to many of us. We continually look to other people, to their apparent accomplishments, and figure that this is the standard by which we judge our life as a success or failure.

I grew up thinking you had to make a mark, always had to be quotable. What I am discovering is that it is possible to be eminently popular with men and failing with God. It is easy to be more concerned with what other people think than what Jesus thinks.

Each of us has a desire for recognition, a desire to be important or influential. Paul calls it the pride of life. It's a desire to be noticeably superior, and it explains our winner complexes and our workaholic natures. We have allowed the world to impose standards of success on us that are not biblical.

Elijah had set an unrealistic standard and he couldn't match it. I'm convinced some servants of God push themselves harder than God ever intended. They are like the old Datsun (Nissan) commercial, "We are driven!" Antacid manufacturers love them. They feel driven to succeed for social acceptance. Maybe you have heard the statement made by a British evangelist, "It is better to burn out than to rust out." That's just not true, because once you burn out there is nothing left to give.

I'm not advocating laziness. I believe strongly in hard work and long hours, but my ministry was beginning to resemble, as mentioned earlier, a circus plate-spinning act. He starts by spinning a few plates on a couple of long, thin wooden poles. Quickly he adds more poles and plates as he runs back and forth to keep the original ones going. The artist is always on the move, trying to keep all the plates spinning simultaneously.

The world record for plate spinning is held by Shukuni Sasaki of Japan. On July 16, 1981, he had 72 plates spinning at the same time.[27] I think there are times in my ministry when I put Shukuni to shame with the number of programs I had spinning. When I wasn't adding more plates to the poles, someone else was adding them for me. I had always felt Christians should be like tea kettles . . . up to their necks in hot water and still singing. Only I had stopped singing.

What I am finding with great regularity is success-driven servants of God whose lives are out of balance. Howard Hendricks notes that in the old days, if you missed a stagecoach that would be okay, you could catch the next one in a month. Today, if you miss a section of a revolving door you're in a tizzy.

After feeding Elijah and allowing him to rest, God asks, "Elijah, what are you doing here?" It's a penetrating question, not a scolding one. God is in the business of restoring failures, those whose lives are out of balance. God nurtured Elijah, gave him wise counsel and made him feel significant again in His plan.

The difference between the finally defeated and the finally successful is not so much that one failed and the other did not. It is the fact that one had the courage to begin again, while the other let one great failure overcome him. As S. I. Hayakawa writes, there is a vast difference between saying, "I have failed three times," and saying, "I am a failure."

Success is doing God's work God's way. As we learn to commit all to Him . . . our jobs, our families, our ministries, ourselves . . . we won't have to worry about being a "success" or a "failure." We only have to concern ourselves with doing what God wants us to do, when He wants us to do it.

When you're down in the dumps, remember God still loves you. You don't love someone who is worthless. You may love someone who is flawed and broken. Just as you love a beat-up old car because you see the original beauty through all the rust and broken glass. God thinks you're special. Isn't it amazing that the world's standard of acceptance is many times much harder than Jesus' standard of acceptance. Jesus accepts you just the way you are.

Remember that mistakes become failures only when we fail to learn from them. Nobody has ever succeeded in life without learning some very important lessons from his mistakes and shortcomings. Failure is part of life. So use your failures; learn from them. We all have known and will know failure. It can continually get us down, or it can make us a stronger and different person.

Try to Prevent Boredom

Youth work tends to be repetitive. Repetitive work loses its creativity. There are several ways to overcome this in volunteers. One way is by not departmentalizing people. Give them a chance to work in a variety of areas of the youth program. For instance, have them teach Sunday school for a year or two, then suggest another area in the youth program—or ask them to think of something new to do, something your youth program hasn't had before.

Another way to prevent boredom is to allow volunteers to take one week off a month. This works great if you have a team of volunteers. We give our Sunday morning Bible school teachers the month of December off and either bring in guest speakers or show films. The teachers can, during this time, go to an adult Bible school class or come and simply listen with no responsibilities in the high-school department.

GIVING YOUR VOLUNTEERS A VISION FOR YOUTH MINISTRY

There is a great difference between being a cutter of stone and a builder of cathedrals, but it is only in vision and perspective. Make sure volunteers see their task as part of the larger ministry of the church. Help volunteers to not get caught in the web of minutiae and miss the joy of being a part of the total mission.

Thomas J. Peters and Robert H. Waterman Jr., in their bestseller *In Search of Excellence,* share this humorous example:

> One individual, early in his career, was receiving instruction as a bank teller. One operation involved hand-sorting eighty-column punched cards, and the woman teaching him could do it as fast as lightning. "Bzzzzzzt" went the deck of cards in her hands, and they were all sorted and neatly stacked. Our friend was all thumbs.
>
> "How long have you been doing this?" he asked her.
>
> "About ten years," she estimated.
>
> "Well," said he, anxious to learn, "what's that operation for?"
>
> "To tell you the truth,"—Bzzzzzzt, another deck sorted—"I really don't know."[28]

157

Beside seeing their ministry as part of the total ministry of the church, volunteers must have a sense of ownership of their ministry. If they don't develop a personal vision for ministry, they'll be tempted to sit back and leave the job to the "hired gun." After all, if they feel like pawns in another person's program instead of being part of a team, why not? Many paid youth ministers control everything. They think their job is to keep things tidy and under control, to issue orders, to make black-and-white decisions, and to treat volunteers as factors of production.

Who Mx?

Xvxn though my typxwritxr is an old modxl, it works wxll, xxcxpt for onx of its kxys. Thxrx arx 41 kxys that function but onx kxy not working makxs thx diffxrxncx. Somxtimxs it sxxms to mx that our staff is not unlikx my typxwritxr—in that not all thx kxys work propxrly. You may say, "Wxll, I am only onx pxrson. I won't makx or brxak our lxadxrship txam." But a succxssful txam, to bx xffxctivx, rxquirxs thx participation of xvxry youth lxadxr. So thx nxxt timx you think your xfforts arx not nxxdxd, rxmxmbxr my old typxwritxr and say to yoursxlf, "I am a kxy pxrson on our txam and I am nxxdxd vxry much. I rxally am important—to thx txam and to our group mxmbxrs."

Yxs Mx![29]

Give volunteers decision-making authority and their motivation will soar. Simply delegating responsibility doesn't foster trust. It often causes friction. Many churches assume the average volunteer worker is incompetent and just itching to mess up. Ever go to a park? Most are peppered with signs that say, "Stay off the grass," "No parking here," "No wading," "No bicycles." A few parks seem to have a different attitude; their signs say: "Campers welcome" or "Picnic tables for your convenience." One park tells you that you shouldn't. The other park says that you should; it urges you to join in and take advantage of the facilities.[30] What kind of park is your church like for your volunteers? The key is trust. We must trust volunteers and help them to see this as *their* ministry.

Psychologists study the need for self-determination in a field called "illusion of control." Stated simply, its findings indicate that if people think they have even a modest personal control over their destinies, they will persist at tasks. They will do better at them. They will become more committed to them. Texas Instrument's Patrick Haggerty says it this way: "Those who implement the plans must make the plans!"[31] Include volunteers in the planning sessions. Ask for their advice and then act on it when you can.

Volunteers are most committed to plans they helped make. People like their own children a lot, and typically aren't that interested in other people's babies. Make certain that they feel this ministry is *their* child and that they aren't merely baby-sitting someone else's. Make sure you provide channels for volunteers to contribute ideas and then encourage them to contribute.

Give your volunteers keys to the buildings. This helps in two areas. One, it shows you trust them and they don't have to come running to you all the time to get in a room. Two— it saves you a lot of time. Guess what it's like to be the only one with a key? Richard Morris in *Ministry: A Magazine for Clergy* indicates the need for ownership of a program:

> As a pastor, I've never been able to get too excited about somebody else's program. Not even if it comes from the conference president. But when it's *my* program, something opens up inside me, and I invest incredible amounts of time and energy to make it work. Why has it taken me so long to see that members of my church are no different? How many years I've wasted trying to get them to do things they had no desire to do, while practically ignoring the potential of their own hopes and dreams concerning their church and their Lord! I think I've finally learned that the right question to ask (as pastor) is not, "How can we get our members to do what we want them to do?" but "How can we help our members fulfill *their own* needs for involvement, commitment, and successful ministry in the church?"[32]

Mary Schramm's book, *Gifts of Grace,* includes the following story that relates directly to our tendency to override the dreams and hopes of our volunteers:

Once a little boy went to school. It was quite a big school, but when the boy found he could go right to his room from the playground outside he was happy, and the school didn't seem quite so big anymore. One morning when the little boy had been in school for a while, the teacher said, "Today we are going to make a picture."

"Good," thought the little boy. He liked to make pictures. He could make lions and tigers and trains and boats. He took out his crayons and began to draw. But the teacher said, "Wait. It's not time to begin." And she waited until everyone looked ready. "Now," said the teacher, "we are going to make flowers."

"Good," thought the little boy, and he began to make beautiful flowers with his orange and pink and blue crayons. But the teacher said, "Wait." She drew a picture on the blackboard. It was red with a green stem. "There, now you may begin."

The little boy looked at the teacher's flower. He liked his better, but he did not say this. He just turned his paper over and made a flower like the teacher's. It was red with a green stem.

On another day the teacher said, "Today we are going to make something with clay." "Good," thought the little boy. He could make all kinds of things with clay—snakes and snowmen and elephants and mice—and he began to pinch and pull his ball of clay. But again the teacher said, "Wait, I'll show you how." And she showed everyone how to make one deep dish. The little boy just rolled his clay in a round ball and made a dish like the teacher's. And pretty soon the little boy learned to wait and to watch and to make things just like the teacher's. And pretty soon he didn't make things of his own anymore.

And then it happened that the little boy and his family moved to another city and the boy had to go to another school. On the very first day he went to school and the teacher said, "Today we are going to make a picture." "Good," thought the boy and he waited for the teacher to tell him what to do. But the teacher didn't say anything. She just walked around the room. When she came to the boy, she said, "Don't you want to make a picture?"

"Yes," said the boy. "What are we going to make?"

"Well, I don't know until you make it," said the teacher.

"How should I make it?" said the boy.

"Why, any way you like!"

"And any color?"

"Any color," said the teacher. "If everyone made the same thing in the same color, how would I know who made what and which was which?"

"I don't know," said the boy, and he began to draw a flower. It was red with a green stem. [33]

WHEN CONFLICTS ARISE (AND THEY WILL)

Conflicts surface in any relationship. When they do, *always clear the air as soon as possible.* It helps to have periodic evaluations with your volunteers; that way, they *know* how they're doing, and there are no surprises. Those review times also give you the opportunity to ask the volunteer what is going well, what needs to be improved, and how you can help.

Volunteers need to know what is expected of them and given regular feedback. Explain up front what their responsibilities will be. Paint them a clear picture; then let them know periodically how they're doing. People want to know where they stand. Even negative feedback is better than no feedback at all. Praise or criticize, but don't ignore. Confront the problem, not the people. Don't get personal unless you have no choice; that can get very painful. Try instead for a positive, nonincriminating discussion of the situation.

Part of being a leader is spending a considerable amount of energy absorbing other people's complaints. It isn't the happiest way to spend one's time, but if a group is to run smoothly people must have an opportunity to get the bile out of their systems. If this sort of ventilation is unpleasant for you, remind yourself that it is one of the ways you keep a group tightly motivated. What we are after is a positive-thinking cadre of people in which there is a minimum of backbiting, criticizing, and negative communication. The

161

only way that will be possible is for the leader to drain off a great deal of venom by getting potential troublemakers aside and hearing them out. Anger is inevitable, and it is much smarter to let it ventilate upward rather than to allow it to smolder down in the ranks. Such smoldering often erupts into a major conflagration. In every group, whether a volunteer staff of four or a company of four hundred, the only way to keep a high level of enthusiasm is to build in adequate corridors for grievances.

In *Bringing out the Best in People*, Alan Loy McGinnis cautions:

> Some congregations never get anything accomplished because the pastor tries to please everyone. The boss who says, "I don't want to hear about the squabbles between you guys— this is for you to work out," is inviting trouble. At times you must go in, hear both sides, push the participants to a compromise, then throw all your weight behind the compromise. The good motivator tries not to lose anyone but also never allows fighting to decimate the organization.[34]

Charles Schulz described the dilemma through his comic strip, *Peanuts*. "Strike three!" the umpire shouts as Lucy is called out on strikes. Sitting on the bench with his manager shirt on, Charlie Brown watches Lucy return to the bench with a ferocious look on her face. Charlie thinks, *Good grief, she struck out again! That's three times so far. . . . I should say something to her. . . . After all, I'm the manager . . . but if I say one word, she'll blow sky high. . . . She's so mad now she's ready to burst . . . I don't dare make a sound. . . . Oh, oh! My throat's getting dry . . . I've got to clear my throat . . . I . . . I . . . gulp! I've got to cough, or go ahem, or something. . . . My throat feels so dry . . . I . . .*

Not being able to stand it any longer, Charlie Brown squeaks, "Ahem." And just as he had thought, Lucy turns to him and screams, "I didn't strike out on purpose!" The scream is so loud it knocks Charlie off the bench and flat on his back. With his cap sideways, circles spinning around his head, and a "what hit me?" look on his face, he says, "We managers have a rough life."[35]

I can identify with Charlie Brown. I've been in a thousand situations where I wanted to speak to a volunteer worker about some problem but felt I couldn't because they would take it the wrong way. Sometimes I've had the courage to plunge in where angels fear to tread—and sometimes I haven't. But regardless of how difficult it may be, supervision is essential if effective work is to be achieved.

If you hand out reprimands, be willing to allow the other person to be unhappy with you for a while. Being an inspiring leader doesn't mean being the smartest or even the hardest-working person in the group. What it does require is that you be firm—firm in your dedication to excellence, even if it makes you temporarily unpopular. Leadership doesn't mean winning popularity contests. "Some of the most talented people are terrible leaders because they have a crippling need to be loved by everyone,"[36] says James Schorr of Holiday Inns. Coach Lombardi's philosophy was this: "I hold it more important to have the players' confidence than their affection."[37] And child psychologist Haim Ginott said, "A good parent must like his children, but he must not have an urgent need to be liked by them every minute of the day."[38]

9.
TURNING THE LIGHTS OFF ... RETIRING VOLUNTEERS

The youth group at one of the churches I served early in my career, in Garden Grove, California, had volunteered to do some service projects for the city. We had already helped distribute food to needy families in the community on Friday afternoon and picked up trash along Chapman Avenue on Saturday morning.

Between the church and the local high school is the Garden Grove Freeway. There is a 10' x 15' tunnel under the freeway to provide access to the school for the students in the community. The tunnel was full of graffiti and drawings. I called the city and volunteered our youth to paint the entire block-long tunnel.

The city was delighted. They ordinarily had to paint the tunnel once or twice a year anyway—and this year they wanted to try a new plan. On Sunday afternoon, they gave us 130 large cans of spray paint—all different colors. We were to spray straight vertical lines up and down on the two side walls of the tunnel. The city figured that, even if someone wrote or drew something on the walls later on, it would be difficult to see and would discourage the vandalism. Twenty-three of us showed up at the tunnel Sunday afternoon. I got our young people started and then left them in the hands of our four adult volunteers, assuming everything would go smoothly.

On Monday morning at 9:00, I received two phone

calls. One from the head of the Parks and Recreation Department; the other from the mayor, asking me to meet them in front of the tunnel at 10:30 A.M. I had never talked to the mayor before and I could tell by the tone of his voice that he was not planning to give me a service award.

In fact, when I arrived at the tunnel, the mayor wanted to lay hands on me—and it was not to ordain me to the ministry. I could not believe my eyes. My kids had not only painted the two walls with stripes as asked . . . but they had also written their own religious graffiti. On the ceiling and outside the tunnel and on the floor of the tunnel were scribbled "God Loves You," "Jesus Is the Answer," "Jesus Saves," and one kid had written fifteen verses from Acts chapter 3! There were also flowers, rainbows, and other samples of high-school art all over the tunnel. The city officials did not appreciate the creativity.

The city had to sandblast the entire tunnel. It took three men two days. For some reason, this was the last project we did for the city, and our adult sponsors had a lot of explaining to do.

DECIDING TO FIRE A VOLUNTEER

And that brings us to a most unpleasant task that every youth worker must face sometime in his ministry: relieving a volunteer of responsibility. Firing him, in other words. It's inevitable—at some point in your career you'll make a mistake (Who, me?) and recruit the wrong person for the wrong ministry or wrong age group. Too many nonfunctional and unhappy volunteers are left in that place of ministry, to everyone's frustration, when they should be relieved of that responsibility and given the opportunity to serve somewhere else.

To be an effective youth ministry leader, you must be both Mr. Nice Guy and Mr. Tough Guy. If you follow professional baseball, you've seen the swings between these two extremes.

Who do you hire for your baseball team when Billy Martin was your last manager? That's easy—you hire Mr. Nice Guy. Billy Martin was tough, demanding, swearing at his players, grabbing them by the shirt, riding them day in and day out. He got results—but after a year and a half, players burn out on that kind of stuff, and the team takes a nosedive in the standings. Martin has had phenomenal results the first two years in each of his managerial tenures.

You follow a guy like that with Mr. Nice Guy. You know—the guy who throws out the balls and bats and says, "Fellas, let's have some fun and play ball." What a relief! The team starts to win again. A year later, under Mr. Nice Guy's management, things become lax. There are no rules, the players start flaking off. Things begin to go downhill. So they bring in a new manager who will have some discipline. Guess who?

If you are either a Mr. Nice Guy or a Mr. Tough Guy, you will have a two-year tenure. To be effective in leadership, you must be able to do either one as needed—to know when to give a pat on the back and when to give a kick in the rump.[1]

Unfortunately, many Christian leaders are Mr. Nice Guy, and their churches go on lazily accomplishing nothing. The question is: When a volunteer fails to meet your expectations or is nonfunctional, are you able to face them one to one and take some definite action? Howard Hendricks said it so clearly: "The test of an executive is how well you can fire. Anyone can hire."[2] There is a vast difference between overlooking an irregularity because you choose to do so in the interest of creativity and, on the other hand, avoiding a problem because you don't like conflict. It is a weak leader who allows morale to be disrupted and the group's work torpedoed because he's afraid to reprimand and dismiss.[3]

Granted, firing must come as a last resort after every effort has been made to salvage the volunteer. Our job, after all, is to redeem people. But sometimes you just have to bite the bullet and do it. Pray for wisdom; think through all the consequences carefully before taking action. Don't use the knee-jerk reaction and just barge in on the person yelling unconfirmed accusations. Sleep on it—or toss and turn on it. Some volunteers will be a cancer in your ministry until they resign or are confronted.

If someone isn't working out in the job he volunteered for, remember: the person isn't wrong—the job is wrong for the person. There's a place for everyone. Think of somewhere else for that person to serve, either within the youth ministry or in another church-related ministry. Even though the volunteer may be disappointed that he won't be allowed to continue in the area he's been involved with, transferring a person from one area of responsibility to another isn't quite the same as firing outright, and doesn't have the same psychological effect.

If the bottom line is that this person must go—if everything reasonably possible has been done to help the volunteer succeed, and due to a lack of willingness or ability the situation continues—then brace yourself and proceed. It's your responsibility. Never lower standards for a volunteer. It is the ultimate put-down for them to feel that what they do is so unimportant that it doesn't matter whether they do it well or even at all. View volunteers as nonpaid staff and always hold them accountable for their commitment. If you love and respect your volunteers, you won't let them continue to do a bad job. And if you don't ask them to step aside, it could be harmful to your young people. You *must* do it, for the volunteers' sake as well as for the young people's.

But be sure you do your homework. You don't want to be challenged publicly and forced to retreat. Get the facts straight. Discuss the problem with an impartial observer, such as the senior pastor, the chairman of the board, or the youth elder.[4] Often, they have a much clearer perception of the situation and can offer some helpful advice and insights.

In approaching the volunteer, don't come as a bolt out of the blue, descending on the unsuspecting volunteer like God's avenging fire. Never let frustration, anger, disappointment, or bitterness build up in you until you can't deal rationally with one of your volunteers. If you've been having periodic review sessions with your volunteers, then the individual you're about to fire should be well aware that you're not very happy with how things are working out. There should be no surprises. This final interview should be conducted eyeball-to-eyeball, face-to-face. Don't say it over the phone or in a letter. Find a neutral location where you won't be disturbed or interrupted.

Mark Senter offers this recollection of his bungled firing of a Sunday school teacher:

> Looking back, I suppose I got what was coming to me. Sending that letter asking Christopher Schwartz to resign as a high school Sunday school teacher wasn't real smart. "Old Chris," as the students called him, deserved better treatment. Yet my stomach knotted every time I thought of confronting Chris with his lack of teaching skills. So I took the chicken way out; I wrote a letter.
>
> Even the kids in Schwartz's class got on my case when they heard what had happened. Not that they liked "Old Chris" as a teacher—they simply felt bad about the way he'd gotten the ax.[5]

With a loving, caring attitude, share with the volunteer honestly in clear, unmistakable terms that he is not working out in this particular area of ministry—and tell him why. Don't forget to point out also all the positive qualities you've seen demonstrated in his life. Don't reject him in a personal sense just because he doesn't fit in one particular niche. Suggest alternative avenues of service ministry.

This is important: After you've had this difficult conversation with a volunteer, *don't ask him to stay on until a replacement is found.* That will just strain your relationship even further and will cause more harm than would just functioning without someone in that position.

The optimistic note is that many volunteers in this situation were *hoping* you would relieve them of the responsibility. They knew they weren't doing a good job; they just didn't know how to approach you. After your discussion, they'll feel like a hundred-pound sack has been lifted from their back—especially if you follow up your talk with affirming, encouraging comments in a brief note or at other get-togethers in the future.

The negative note is that it isn't always this pleasant or easy. I had a group of adult volunteers involved in a particular area of our church's youth ministry who weren't compatible. Whenever they were together, there was always tension, bitterness, and ill feeling—which, of course, spilled over and was very visible during youth meetings. I met with them individually several times to no avail. They were all high-strung, aggressive people. They were fine by themselves, but the chemistry didn't gel when they were together. It was getting so bad that the young people were coming to me to pray about the behavior of these adults!

It's sad when the kids are more mature than their adult leaders. After clearing it with our elders, I closed down that section of our ministry. Some of the volunteers were relieved, but some were angry and resentful. They were so vocal, in fact, that I thought I might even lose my job. I'm not sure, looking back, that I handled all of it correctly, but I knew it had to be done. Time does heal wounds, and these adults are still in the church; I don't feel like hiding when I see them coming. In fact, I consider them to be my friends. But it was not a pleasant experience.

AFTER YOU'VE FIRED A VOLUNTEER

Firing a volunteer may make you unpopular with the youth group—and maybe even with the congregation. People may be angry with you. That old feeling of isolation may creep in.

If you find yourself feeling alone after giving somebody

the ax, here are eight tips as shared by Brad Wesner in *Group* that will help:

1. Remember God is still there; you aren't alone. God loves you and will listen to you.

2. Find someone, maybe another youth minister, who can relate to your feelings. Talk it out.

3. If you can't find even one friendly ear, write your thoughts; they're begging to be expressed.

4. When the final decision has been made, don't stew over it; you can't change it. Focus on something else.

5. Do something constructive with your time. Avoid staring at walls and ceilings. Go to a movie, do a craft, write a letter, read a book or magazine.

6. Avoid feeling sorry for yourself; pity only worsens the situation.

7. Remember that your friends still like you; they're angry because of the issue, not because you're a creep.

8. Attend a public event, like a basketball game. That'll keep you in touch with people and also keep your mind off your loneliness.[6]

10.
GREAT IDEAS ON THE CARE AND FEEDING OF VOLUNTEERS

These outstanding ideas about how to build relationships between volunteers and kids appeared first in the forty-one volumes of *Ideas* books published by Youth Specialties, Inc., in El Cajon, California. Not all are appropriate for every group, of course, so choose carefully which ones to use with your volunteers and adapt these ideas as necessary to fit the needs of your group.

STAFF STUMPERS
Here's a fun game that will really help kids get to know the staff (youth director, youth sponsors, advisors, and teachers) a lot better. Before the game have each staff member answer (with short answers) a list of questions like these:

1. Why are you on the staff?
2. What has been your most embarrassing moment while "on the job" with the youth?
3. If you could go anywhere in the world, where would it be?
4. What makes you happy?
5. Who has had the most influence on your life?
6. Who is your favorite performer?
7. If you had a million dollars, what would you do with it?

8. My dream is to . . . (complete sentence).
9. What has been the best book that you have read recently (excluding the Bible)?
10. What is your favorite scripture verse?

After each staff member has filled out the questionnaire, create a multiple-choice quiz using their answers and print up enough copies for everybody. Ask the kids to guess which staff member gave which answer by writing the staff member's initials after the choice. The answers should be in a different order for each question. For example, question number three might look like this:

3. If you could go anywhere in the world, where would it be?
_____ a. The French Riviera
_____ b. The Holy Land
_____ c. Home
_____ d. Butte, Montana
_____ e. Hawaii

After the kids have made their guesses, the staff members can come to the front, and each answer the questions correctly. The kids can then check their papers to see just how well they know their staff.

TEEN OF THE WEEK

Here's a great way to make your kids feel important and also to help your volunteer staff become better acquainted with the kids. Each week choose a Teen of the Week who is the honored guest at that week's youth meeting.

First, choose the lucky teen. Then have one of the adult volunteers or staff prepare to tell that teen's life history. Contact the chosen teen's parents secretly and have them provide you with family photos, baby pictures, awards, report cards, toys, articles of clothing, or anything that would be of interest to the group. Display these items on a bulletin board set aside as the Teen of the Week board. When the young people arrive for the meeting, they will see who is

Teen of the Week. In addition, honor the chosen young person in some special way during the meeting. It's a good way to have fun and to let each kid know he's special.

And, of course, you can also do the same for your adult volunteers: "Youth Staff of the Week."

YOUTH SPONSOR'S MYSTERY NIGHT

No single event in youth ministry is as important as close, personal contact with youth, and there is no better way than by giving yourself and your time and creating a little mystery about yourself. Kids love to stay overnight at friends' homes—why not at the youth sponsor's house? Invite four to six kids to spend a Mystery Night at your house. Have them bring sleeping bags and sleep in your living room. Go to a movie and for pizza, then let them fall asleep watching your TV and talking to their friends. In this setting, a bond can form not only between youth and adult but also between youth who had previously not known each other well or between "in" youth and "out" youth. Don't let the simplicity of this event fool you; its benefits can be surprising.

GET STARTED AND GET ACQUAINTED

This idea is designed to help newly-recruited youth sponsors and advisors have more personal interaction with kids in the youth group. Most volunteer adult sponsors work full-time and don't have time to "hang-out" with the kids at their events and favorite places.

Early in the school year, plan some time for each youth sponsor to have dinner (at their home, if possible) with small groups of kids, just to get to know them better. Give the sponsors a list of questions, which will provide insight into personality and background, to ask each young person. Some sponsors might find it more convenient to take kids to breakfast or go on a picnic lunch. Money for food expenses might be provided from your youth budget.

175

After these dinners, perhaps over a period of a month, schedule a get-together. Include a lighthearted roast, a time of sharing some of the things said and done at the dinners.

GROUP BASEBALL CARDS

Collecting baseball cards is still one of America's favorite pastimes. Now there are companies that will make custom baseball cards that feature student athletes for high schools and colleges. Here are all kinds of possibilities for the creative youth worker.

Customize baseball cards for your youth group. Cards can include picture and name on one side and such vital statistics as age, grade, likes and dislikes, right- or left-handed, and "batting average" on the other side. Some of the cards can feature members of your volunteer staff. Besides being fun to collect and trade, these cards help kids and the volunteer staff get to know each other better.

These cards can be printed locally and financed by selling advertising space (in small print) on the back of the cards. Each kid gets a stack of his own cards and trades until he has everyone else's card in his collection. Or give each young person a complete set of cards to begin with.

As a variation, take photos of all the athletes at your local high school, get the information you need, and print up decks of cards to be sold or given to the student body. Include a Bible verse or a positive slogan from your church or youth group. The possibilities are unlimited.

PHOTO BLOWUPS

Here's a good idea for this year's grad night celebration. Collect all your graduates' senior pictures or any good portrait photo and have giant poster-sized blowups made with a professional-looking name tag underneath each one to decorate the room. The result is quite impressive, and the posters make nice gifts for each grad when the celebration is over.

Check the telephone directory for photo studios in your area that will do this or write: Wallet Photo Co., P.O. Box 2000, Dept. 473, West Caldwell, NJ 07006. This company will make posters from small photos by mail order for a surprisingly low cost.

FAMILY PICTURES

This idea is useful for providing a sense of belonging in the youth group and for dividing up the kids for classes, activities, or work projects. The entire youth group is divided into families, groups of eight to twelve kids. Each family has a spiritual mom and dad, the youth sponsors, and a family name. These families can be divided according to age groups, schools, geographical locations (where they live), or any other way you choose. To help solidify these families, take family pictures with each family dressing according to a theme of their choice, such as in old-fashioned clothes, formal attire, hillbilly outfits, army fatigues, or athletic gear. Print the pictures in the church paper and in youth group postcards or display them on the youth bulletin board.

YMTV

Home video is gaining in popularity as the equipment becomes cheaper and easier to use. Create your own video library featuring special youth concerts, fellowships, dramas, and other activities for future viewing. Borrow a video camera from someone in your youth ministry. When you host singing groups, speakers, and other special guests, videotape them (with their permission, of course) and then allow the kids to check out the video cassettes whenever they want to see them again. Many young people are into MTV (Music Television), so call yours YMTV—Youth Ministry Television!

YOUTH LEADER'S COUPON BOOK

Most youth workers can't afford to give every young person in their group a Christmas or birthday present.

Here's a gift idea that is economical as well as valuable. Create a coupon book that offers a variety of services to the young people and is redeemable any time during the year. Think up as many coupons as you like.

- Good for one free dinner at my house
- Good for one free "rap session." Void between 11:00 P.M. and 7:00 A.M.
- Good for prayer for any prayer request.
- Good for one free ride (in an emergency) to the destination of your choice (within reason).
- Good for one "encouraging word." Redeemable any time.
- Good for one free "Pat on the Back" when needed.
- Good for one pretty good answer to your most burning question.
- Good for one treasure map: A free treasure will be given to anyone who visits the youth pastor's office Monday through Friday between 9:00 A.M. and 4:30 P.M. Call for an appointment.

These coupons not only offer the kids something for free, they also make them aware of the kinds of things you're willing to do for them.

SPONSOR PAINTING

This crazy idea is best used at the beginning of the year when introducing new youth sponsors to the group, although it could take place anytime. The youth sponsors hide, and the group divides into the same number of groups as there are sponsors. At a signal, each group holds hands and, as a group, tries to locate one of the sponsors. Once they find one, they bring him back to a central location where there is a supply of watercolor paint and brushes. Each group paints designs on the youth sponsor's face, arms, and legs. Award prizes for the most creative designs.

PICTURE POSTCARDS

To communicate with kids in your group or make newcomers feel more included, use a 35mm camera and take several pictures of each young person and some group pictures, as well as newcomers too. Order jumbo-sized prints when you get the film developed.

When you need to communicate, send these photos as postcards with message, name and address, and stamp on the back. These are instantly personal and fun to receive.

STICKER POSTCARDS

Here's a quick way to create your own personalized postcards to send members. Go to any stationery or art supply store and purchase a variety of stickers with positive messages like "Good Work!" or "Terrific!" or "U-R-Tops!" They're usually available individually or in rolls or sheets. Use them to add color to ordinary, drab postcards. Add a personal note, and you've got a great way to encourage and congratulate your kids.

THE THOUGHTFUL VOLUNTEER

You can develop some lasting relationships with kids in your group by taking time each week to send personal thank-you notes to any kids who helped or participated in a special way during the last week. Use notepaper with your name printed on it. Write new kids and thank them for coming, thank the old-timers for bringing a guest, or thank kids for such little things as helping to set up chairs or participating in a discussion. Also, send a birthday card that you have obviously selected especially for each kid. The results of your thoughtfulness will surprise you.

GENERIC GREETING CARDS

It's always a good idea to remember your young people by sending them birthday cards, get-well cards, and thank-you cards; however, keeping an inventory of all those cards can put a strain on storage space.

Create your own Generic Card, printed on yellow paper (like all those yellow-brand products in the grocery store). Serving as an all-purpose card, it's a good way to let kids know you care about them, and the kids enjoy receiving them. Of course, you'll want to add a personal note on the back when you send it.

Here's how to design it:

DUD POSTCARDS

Chances are you have or have access to lots of old snapshots that didn't turn out. Maybe the setting on your camera wasn't quite right or you cut off somebody's head. No matter what the circumstance, these old photos make excellent postcards—especially the jumbo-sized ones. Just write a personal note (making reference to the wonderful photo, of course) on it, address it, stamp it, and mail it. Kids love to receive these unique, one-of-a-kind picture postcards.

PURPLE HEART AWARD

Here's a thoughtful and humorous way to encourage and thank an adult youth sponsor after a particularly difficult or demanding activity. Present him with a Purple Heart Award that bears an inscription similar to this: "In recognition for service above and beyond the call of duty in Youth Ministry."

The award can be made out of purple construction paper and framed. You can even have a presentation ceremony. Your sponsors will enjoy the attention and appreciate your thoughtfulness.

FUN FACT SHEET

It's always a good idea to keep up-to-date information on all the kids who attend your youth group meetings. Here's a form that works well for finding out a few pertinent facts to use for planning and getting kids involved, as well as a visitor's registration form for first-timers. (See page 182.)

WELCOME!

Here's a good way to welcome a new staff member at the church, a new youth sponsor, or a new young person in the group. Have all the kids write a letter to the new person introducing themselves and enclosing a free coupon. For example, the coupon might say, "I will deliver a pie on your request," or "If you want two free guitar lessons, call me," or "I'll buy lunch for you any Saturday." Then, all the letters and coupons are presented to the newcomer, who really feels wanted and accepted.

WELCOME! PART TWO

Another way to help a new person feel welcome, especially those who are newcomers to your area, is to ask

WELCOME

NAME _____

ADDRESS_____

CITY _____ ZIP _____

SCHOOL _____YEAR _____

PHONE NUMBER _____

_____I WOULD LIKE TO KNOW ABOUT THIS GROUP'S ACTIVITIES.

_____I WOULD LIKE TO KNOW ABOUT THE BIBLE STUDIES.

_____I CAME WITH A FRIEND.

_____I CAME WITH MY FAMILY.

_____I CAME ON MY OWN.

_____I CAME BECAUSE MY PARENTS MADE ME.

_____I CAME BY ACCIDENT.

_____I WORK AT _____

_____I DON'T WORK, BUT WISH I DID.

_____I DON'T WORK, AND HOPE I NEVER WILL.

_____AT SCHOOL I'M INVOLVED IN _____

_____

_____I DON'T ATTEND ANOTHER CHURCH

_____I ATTEND _____ CHURCH

          _____OFTEN

          _____NEVER

          _____NOW & THEN

I LIKE TO:

_____H$_2$O SKI	_____BASEBALL
_____SNOW SKI	_____FRISBEE
_____READ	_____SEW
_____DRAMA	_____PAINT
_____BASKETBALL	_____DRIVE CRAZILY
_____VOLLEYBALL	_____BACKPACK
_____SOCCER	_____ROCK CLIMB
_____FOOTBALL	_____HANG AROUND & BE COOL
_____CHESS	_____PICK MY NOSE
_____SKATEBOARD	_____PICK MY FRIEND'S NOSE
_____RUN	_____GET STRAIGHT A's
_____LOOK AT GUYS	_____SPIT ON PEOPLE WHO GET STRAIGHT A's
_____EAT	_____TENNIS
_____LOOK AT GIRLS	_____SWIM
_____LISTEN TO MUSIC	_____SURF
_____WRITE ON BATHROOM WALLS	_____ROLLERSKATE
_____READ BATHROOM WALLS	_____GOLF
_____WORK ON CARS	_____FILL OUT LONG QUESTIONNAIRES

your group to answer the following questionnaire. After the kids have answered all the questions, give the survey results to the new person or plan a discussion time and use the survey questions as the topic. Here are some sample questions:

1. Where can you get the best and cheapest hamburgers in town?
2. Where is the best place to just sit and talk?
3. What's the best radio station?
4. Where is the least expensive movie theater?
5. Where do you go if you want to run into your friends?
6. What should a person be sure and not miss if he can only spend one day in our town?
7. What's the best thing about our youth group?
8. What's the best event that our youth group does every year?

ROTATING PLANNING SESSION

Most kids dread boring planning sessions. Here's a great way to add a little excitement and enthusiasm for planning with large groups. Divide your entire group into small groups of four. Place tables all around the room and assign each of the tables a Brainstorm Topic, such as Discussion Topics, Recreation Ideas, Fund-raising Projects, and Service Projects. Each group sits at one of the tables with pencil and paper. At the sound of a buzzer or whistle, each group has just five minutes to write down as many ideas as they can. When the whistle blows again, each group moves to another table in a clockwise direction and writes ideas on the new topic.

To add to the fun, challenge the groups to see which group can think of the most ideas for any one topic and award prizes. At the conclusion of this planning game, you'll find that you have tons of ideas and that the boring planning session wasn't so boring after all.

WEEKLY PLANNING SHEET

If you have trouble getting organized each week for your youth group meetings and activities, try a weekly planning sheet. (See page 185.) It will help you, as well as others, think through what needs to be done. Fill it out and give copies to your youth advisors, the pastor, and youth council. The following planning sheet is only a suggested format, though it has been used with good results. Create your own to fit the needs of your program.

PLANNING SURVEY

Using a survey like the one on page 188 can be very helpful at the beginning of the school year in planning programs and activities. Not only will you get a good idea of what the needs and likes of your kids are, but it gives them more of a feeling of participation in the planning of activities. Print the survey, distribute it, and allow the kids to work on it for as long as necessary. After you get the results, discuss them with all the kids as well as with your leaders to begin planning.

EVENT RESPONSE SHEET

Building a consistent youth ministry is a constant yearly challenge. One help for steady improvement is the use of an Event Response Sheet. (See page 189.) The key to its effectiveness is recording your data after each event for future planning and evaluating the results when you decide to repeat an event or try to develop a new one. The response sheet must be general enough to cover youth events from a service project to a fellowship banquet to a retreat. This is a good way to involve more people in the youth ministry as you continually provide feedback to your program.

YOUTH EVENING PLAN SHEET   DATE:_____

NAME:_____

TIME
ALLOCATION   GOAL FOR THE EVENING:_____   PHONE #:_____

MEAL PREPARED BY:_____

ANNOUNCEMENTS:_____

ACTIVITY:_____

        1. MATERIALS NEEDED:_____

        2. COST:_____   PHONE #:_____

        3. TRANSPORTATION BY:_____

SONGS:_____

SCRIPTURE TO STUDY:_____   PURPOSE:_____

TITLE:_____

FURTHER EXPRESSIONS OF WORSHIP:_____

LESSON OUTLINE:_____

_____

_____

ALTERNATE BACKUP ACTIVITY:_____

        1. MATERIALS NEEDED:_____

        2. COST:_____

THINGS I NEED TO DO FOR NEXT WEEK:_____

PEOPLE I NEED TO BE WITH OR PHONE:_____

CONCERNS I NEED TO PRAY FOR:_____

YOUTH'S RESPONSES TO THE EVENING:_____

CREATIVE THOUGHTS AND IDEAS FOR THE FUTURE:_____

EVENING RATING

1 2 3 4 5 6 7 8 9 10

                        EXCELLENT

PITIFUL

FIFTY PHRASES TO BURY A NEW IDEA

Next time you have a planning session, give all your leaders the following list ahead of time. Tell them that you just want them to come "prepared." Chances are they will be less likely to use any of these phrases regarding new ideas you discuss:

1. We tried that before.
2. Our church is different.
3. It costs too much.
4. That's beyond our responsibility.
5. That's not my job.
6. We're all too busy to do that.
7. It's too radical a change.
8. We don't have the time.
9. Not enough help.
10. Let's do research first.
11. Not practical.
12. The congregation will never buy it.
13. Bring it up in six months.
14. We've never done it before.
15. Christians don't do that.
16. We don't have the authority.
17. That's too ivory tower.
18. Let's get back to reality.
19. That's not our problem.
20. Why change it, it's still working okay
21. I don't like the idea.
22. You're right, but . . .
23. You're two years ahead of your time.
24. We're not ready for that.
25. We don't have the money, equipment, room, personnel.
26. It isn't in the budget.
27. Can't teach an old dog new tricks.
28. Good thought, but impractical.
29. Let's hold it in abeyance.
30. Let's give it more thought.
31. The elders would never go for it.
32. That's what liberals (fundamentalists . . .) do.
33. Not that again.
34. Where'd you dig that one up?
35. We did all right without it.

36. It's never been tried before.
37. It would take away from our missions emphasis.
38. Let's form a committee.
39. Parents won't like it.
40. I don't see the connection.
41. It won't work in our church.
42. What you are really saying is . . .
43. Our denomination doesn't do it that way.
44. Don't you think we should look into it further before we act?
45. Remember, this is a church.
46. It can't be done.
47. It's too much trouble to change.
48. I know a church who tried it.
49. We've always done it this way.
50. It isn't on the agenda.

TWELVE COMMANDMENTS OF YOUTH WORK

The following Twelve Commandments are actually twelve ways to make sure your youth group goes down the drain, but it is also a helpful list of no-no's for any good youth worker. You may want to hang it on your office wall.

1. WIPE OUT INCENTIVE. Tell your kids that someone tried their ideas six years ago. It didn't work then, and it won't work now!

2. DEPEND ON ONLY A FEW TEENS. Use a few pets for every activity and privilege. Don't try to develop responsibility in others.

3. DO NOT COMMEND YOUR TEENS. Take them and their efforts for granted.

4. REPRIMAND YOUR TEENS FOR WEAK-NESSES. Never bother to pray that they will be strengthened. Just scold them for their faults.

5. EXPECT EVERYONE TO CONFORM TO YOUR WAY OF THINKING. This covers everything! Whatever might happen—you are always right!

TOPICS Circle 10 that most interest you.	METHODS Circle 4 that you most enjoy.	RECREATION Circle 8 that you most enjoy.	SERVICE PROJECTS Circle 6 which you most want to do.
1. Alcohol 2. Anger 3. Bible Studies 4. Competition 5. Careers 6. Colleges 7. Dating 8. Death 9. Drugs 10. Ecology 11. Faith 12. Getting Along with Brothers & Sisters 13. Getting Along with Parents 14. Getting Along with Friends 15. Getting Along with Adults 16. God's Will 17. Group Pressure 18. Hunger 19. Identity 20. Independence 21. Jealousy 22. Love 23. Marriage 24. Poverty/Affluence 25. Religion 26. Race 27. Sex 28. School 29. Suburbia 30. Women's Lib 31. World Religions 32. Values Others: 33. _____ 34. _____ 35. _____	1. Skits 2. Puppets 3. Making Banners 4. Discussion 5. Rapping 6. Panel 7. Movies 8. Film Strip 9. Role Playing 10. Speaker 11. Group Study 12. Workbooks Others: 13. _____ 14. _____ 15. _____	1. Beach 2. City Park 3. Skiing 4. Softball 5. Volleyball 6. Kickball 7. Over the Line 8. Bike Hike 9. Swimming 10. Progressive Dinner 11. Pizza Pary 12. Horseback Riding 13. Miniature Golf 14. Tubing 15. Go-carts 16. Bowling 17. Trampolines 18. Roller Skating 19. Ice Skating 20. Dance/Disco 21. Cookout 22. Hayride 23. Square Dancing 24. Canoeing Others: 25. _____ 26. _____ 27. _____	1. Fix Up Youth Room 2. Christmas Caroling 3. Trick-or-Treat for UNICEF 4. Spook House for UNICEF 5. Car Wash for World Hunger 6. Visit Nursing Home 7. Thanksgiving Baskets 8. Tour a United Fund Agency 9. Collect Aluminum Cans 10. Newspaper Drive 11. Visit Prospective Church Members 12. Cook Meal for Congregation to Raise Money for Retreats 13. Sponsor Drop-in Center for Neighborhood Youth 14. Adopt an Orphan Overseas Others: 15. _____ 16. _____ 17. _____ 18. _____

6. DON'T TRY TO DEVELOP GROUP SPIRIT AND MORALE AMONG YOUR TEENS. Why waste precious time developing traits that should have been developed long ago.

7. DO NOT SPEND TIME WITH THEM PERSONALLY. Tell them you are too busy to listen to their problems; besides, you have enough problems of your own.

8. BETRAY CONFIDENCES. Use a confidence given to you by one of your young people as an illustration in your youth meeting.

9. SET UP A SPY SYSTEM. Ask your pets to report any "questionable" things going on among their friends. It will foster doubt and mistrust (to say nothing of disunity).

EVENT RESPONSE SHEET

1. Evaluation for project, activity, or study _____

2. Date _____

3. Grade in school and sex of youth _____ _____ M or F

Scoring Key:
90-100 Strongly agree or Yes!
80-90 Mildly agree
70-80 Disagree
60-70 Strongly disagree or No!   Score

I. *"Build-up"*—Were you aware of the event? How well were you   _____
informed? Did you have adequate time to prepare to participate in the
event?

II. *Objectives*—Did you understand what was trying to be accomplished?   _____
Was it clear to you what was going on?

III. *Value*—Was the event valuable? Was it worth participating in? Was it   _____
something you thought was important that youth should consider?

IV. *Interest*—Did it meet a need or interest that you have? Did it benefit you   _____
in your Christian growth? Was it helpful to Christian living?

V. *Leadership*—Did the leaders seem prepared? Did they present the   _____
material thoroughly? Did you feel they tried to do a good job?

VI. *Repeatability*— Would you recommend repeating this event again? Do   _____
you think an annual event of this type would be good?

OUTSTANDING FACTORS:

AREAS TO IMPROVE UPON:

---

10. BLAME YOUR FAILURE AS A LEADER ON THE KIDS. We will let you define this point yourself—no one knows better than you who is really to blame.

11. MAKE CHRISTIANITY A RELIGION OF DON'TS. Be sure to capitalize on all of the no-no's of Christianity. That is much easier than teaching that the Christian life is a healthy, disciplined freedom, offering opportunity for our own self-expression and assumption of responsibilities.

12. BE A GRUMP. No one likes anyone better than an

all-around grump. It does wonders for the morale and spirit of the entire group!

GROUP MASCOT

One good way to build identity and unity in your youth group is to adopt a mascot. First make up a funny name, such as WUMY (Wesley United Methodist Youth). Then announce a contest to design the mascot and generate lots of ideas. Have the youth vote on the best design.

At future meetings, make T-shirts for the group using liquid embroidery or a silk screen. You can also have patches made for ski caps, jackets, baseball caps, or any other team identity the group might want. Once the design is established it can have all kinds of uses—stuffed animals, needlepoint, stationery, and posters. As a good morale raiser for your kids, a mascot can also help the group feel an increased sense of unity.

YOUTH GROUP HOTLINE

Here's a good way to keep your group informed about upcoming events and give them a way to leave messages for you. Invest in an answering machine and ask the phone company to give you a private number for it. Change the message daily with news of upcoming events, a thought for the day, or jokes. Invite kids to leave a message in the allotted time. You will find that both the young people and their parents will use this hotline a lot.

CHECKLIST FOR THE SPECIAL EVENT

To save a lot of headaches when planning a special event, here's a checklist to ensure that you don't have any little surprises when it's time for the event.

SPECIAL EVENT CHECKLIST

What's happening? _____

Date(s)? _____ Time(s) or Schedule _____

Alternative date(s) _____

Where? _____

Special Preparations _____

Special Equipment _____

Who is it happening for? _____ Est. No. _____

Can they bring friends? _____

Is there a charge? How much? _____ per _____

If profit-making, who gets it? _____
Donation _____ To Whom? _____
How much? _____ %

Is there a registration slip and/or parental permission slip? _____

Who will type/write it? _____

Is there a limited number who may register? _____
If yes, how many _____

Who is responsible for contacting those invited? _____

Media _____ By what date? _____
(L) Letter   (B) Bulletin   (N) Weekly Net News
(P) Phone   (C) Community   (PC) Postcard
(M) Bulk Mailing to Youth   (O) Other, specify _____

Return to whom? _____
Address _____

Make check payable to _____

Emergency number(s) _____
To be published? _____

Is there a money break for early registration? _____
By _____ How much? _____ Refunds? _____

Any specific rules/regulations? (list) _____

Transportation plans? _____

    Cost? _____ Who pays? _____ Organizer? _____

Should plans be in contact media? _____

    If yes, details _____

Accommodations necessary? _____

    Cost? _____ Who pays? _____ Organizer? _____

Meals/Food? _____

    Cost? _____ Who pays? _____ Organizer? _____

Special purchases necessary? _____

    Who will get? _____ By? _____

Special equipment participants must bring? _____

Cleanup? _____ Who is responsible? _____

Should participants be notified to bring
extra money? _____
Amt. _____

"Spiritual" aspects _____

    Who is responsible? _____

Does happening require adult chaperones? _____

    If so, how many? _____ Who will get them? _____

    By what date? _____

Which youth(s) are directly responsible for putting this happening
together? _____

Do any adult official(s) have to be notified? _____

    If yes, who? _____

    Position _____

    Who will notify? _____ By? _____

Must any special form(s) be filled out? _____

    If yes, which forms? _____

    Who will fill out? _____ By? _____

Notes

INTRODUCTION

1. Harold S. Kushner, *When All You Ever Wanted Isn't Enough* (New York: Summit Books, 1986), p. 150.
2. Len Kageler, *The Manual* (16874 First Avenue N.W., Seattle, Washington 98177, 1984), p. 72.
3. David Roadcup, *Methods For Youth Ministry* (Cincinnati, Ohio: Standard Publishing, 1986), p. 63. "Developing Adult Leaders," by Dick Alexander.
4. Marlene Wilson, *How To Mobilize Church Volunteers* (Minneapolis: Augsburg Publishing House, 1983), p. 17.
5. Adapted from a message given by Oswald Hoffman at Billy Graham Evangelistic Training Seminar, Anaheim, California, July 1985.

CHAPTER ONE

1. Les Christie, *Getting A Grip On Time Management* (Wheaton, Ill.: Victor Books, 1984), p. 6.
2. "Geese," *Campus Life Magazine* (Christianity Today, Inc., 1975).
3. *Rocky* (MGM/United Artists 1976), Sylvester Stallone to Talia Shire.
4. Ray Willey, *Working With Youth* (Wheaton, Ill.: Victor Books, 1982), p. 35.
5. Kenneth McGuire, "Belaying—A Model for Ministry," *Leadership*, Vol. III, no. 3 (Summer 1982): 47.
6. Barbara Bracey and Robert Stebe, *Identity, Intimacy, Power* (Phoenix, Arizona: Orangewood Presbyterian Church, 1985), p. 14.
7. *Ibid.*, p. 46.
8. Mary R. Schramm, *Gifts of Grace* (Minneapolis: Augsburg Publishing House, 1982), p. 64.
9. J. B. Phillips, *The Young Church In Action* (New York: MacMillan, 1955), p. 7.
10. Wilson, *How To Mobilize Church Volunteers*, p. 15–16.
11. Albert McCellan, *The New Times: A Prophetic Look At The Challenge of the Christian Church in the 1970's.*

12. Paul Fleischmann, *Discipling the Young Person* (San Bernardino, Calif.: Here's Life Publishers, 1985) p. 14.

CHAPTER TWO

1. Greg McKinnon, "Why Youth Workers Sabotage Volunteers," *Youth Worker*, Vol. II, no. IV (Winter 1986): 22.
2. *Ibid.*, p. 23.
3. Wilson, *How To Mobilize Church Volunteers*, p. 35.
4. *Ibid.*, p. 51
5. Jill Briscoe, *Here Am I, Send Aaron* (Wheaton, Ill.: Victor Books, 1978), p. 39.
6. Eugene C. Kennedy, "The Parachute," *You* (May 2, 1974).
7. *The Effective Management of Volunteer Programs* (Volunteer Management Associates, 1976), p. 102.
8. Noel Becchetti, "Are You a Volunteer Destroyer?" *Youth Worker*, Vol. II, no. IV (Winter 1986): 26.

CHAPTER THREE

1. Dick Alexander, quoted from a message given at the National Youth Leaders Convention, Joplin, Missouri, January 1982.
2. *Webster's New Collegiate Dictionary* (Springfield, Mass.: A Merriam-Webster Co., 1977), p. 904.
3. Wilson, *How to Mobilize Church Volunteers*, p. 108.
4. Elizabeth O'Connor, *Letters to Scattered Pilgrims*, (New York: Harper & Row, 1982).
5. Foster, *Celebration of Discipline*, pp. 112–113.
6. John MacArthur, quoted from a message given at Forest Home Christian Conference Center, April 1976.
7. Mickey Cox and John Denney, *Grab Bag/Resources for Youth Ministry*, "Liking as a Channel of Communication" by Les Shelton (Kansas City, Mo.: Beacon Hill Press), p. 20.
8. David Roadcup, quoted from a message given at National Youth Leaders Convention, Joplin, Missouri, 1980.
9. *The Great Santini* (Orion Pictures/Warner Bros., 1979), Michael O'Keefe to Robert Duval.
10. Wayne Rice, *Junior High Ministry* (Grand Rapids, Mich.: Zondervan Publishing House, 1978), pp. 32–34.

11. MacArthur, message.
12. Paul Fleischmann, *Discipling the Young Person* (San Bernardino, Calif.: Here's Life Publishers, 1985) p. 22.
13. David Roadcup, *Recruiting, Training, and Developing Volunteer Youth Workers* (Cinncinnati, Ohio: Standard Publishing, 1987).
14. Rice, *Junior High Ministry,* pp. 28–31.
15. David Elkind, *All Grown Up & No Place to Go,* (Reading, Mass.: Addison-Wesley, 1984), pp. 45–67.
16. *Washington Post,* October 31, 1986.
17. Cox and Denney, *Grab Bag/Resources for Youth Ministry,* "Bake Sale" by Wes Seeliger, p. 14.
18. Alexander, message.
19. Bill Reif, quoted from a message given at National Youth Workers Convention, 1985.
20. Cox and Denney, *Grab Bag/Resources for Youth Ministry,* "Liking as a Channel of Communication" by Les Shelton, p. 20.
21. Tim Coop, *Youth Sponsors Survival Kit* (Corona, Calif.: Crossroads Christian Church, Box 567, 1977), p. 12.
22. Pat Hurley, *The Penetrators* (Wheaton, Ill.: Victor Books, 1978), pp. 45–46.
23. Wilson, *How To Mobilize Church Volunteers,* p. 59.
24. Wes Seeliger, *Faith At Work* (March 1974): 17.
25. David Roadcup, *Methods For Youth Ministry,* p. 64.
26. Len Kageler, *The Manual,* p. 85.
27. *Ibid.,* p. 86.
28. *Ibid.,* pp. 57–58.

CHAPTER FOUR

1. Cox and Denney, *Grab Bag/Resources for Youth Ministry,* "If I Were You and You Were Me" by Norm Shoemaker, p. 14.
2. J. David Stone and Rose Mary Miller, *Volunteer Youth Workers* (Loveland, Colo.: Group Books, 1985), p. 57.
3. Darrell Pearson, *Parents as Partners in Youth Ministry* (Wheaton, Ill.: Victor Books, 1985), pp. 28–31.
4. *Ibid.*

CHAPTER FIVE

1. Len Kageler, *The Manual,* p. 49.
2. John Hall, "Ten Wrong Ways to Recruit Volunteers," *Youth Worker,* Vol. II, no. IV (Winter 1986): 48.
3. Wilson, *How To Mobilize Church Volunteers,* p. 53.
4. Steve and Cora Alley, *Children's Ministry Manual* (1984), p. 28.
5. Scott Koenigsaecker, "How Do You Spell Volunteer?" *Youth Worker,* Vol. II, no. IV (Winter 1986): 29.
6. *Ibid.,* p. 30.
7. Mark Senter III, *The Art of Recruiting Volunteers* (Wheaton, Ill.: Victor Books, 1983), pp. 87–88.
8. Lyle E. Schaller, "Enlisting Volunteers," *Leadership,* Vol. III, no. 3 (Summer 1982): 60.
9. Senter, *The Art of Recruiting Volunteers,* p. 92.
10. Schaller, "What Does No Mean?" *Leadership,* Vol. III, no. 3 (Summer, 1982) p. 48.
11. Bill McNabb, Associate Minister at Brentwood Presbyterian Church, shared this idea at a Youth Specialties planning meeting.

CHAPTER SIX

1. Lee Sparks, "Finding and Keeping Good Adult Sponsors," *The Youth Group How-To Book* (Loveland, Colo.: Group Books), p. 17.
2. John L. Carroll and Keith L. Ignatius, *Youth Ministry Sunday, Monday and Everyday* (Valley Forge, Pa.: Judson Press, 1972), p. 41.

CHAPTER SEVEN

1. David O. Moberg, *The Church as a Social Institution,* (Englewood Cliffs, N.J.: Prentice-Hall, Inc., 1962), p. 416.
2. Roadcup, *Recruiting, Training, and Developing Volunteer Youth Workers.*
3. Steve and Cora Alley, *Children's Ministry Manual,* (1984), p. 28.
4. Bracey and Stebe, *Identity, Intimacy, Power,* pp. 16–18.
5. Roadcup, *Recruiting, Training, and Developing Volunteer Youth Workers.*

6. Mike West, "Developing a Volunteer Team," in *The Youth Leaders Source Book,* Gary Dausey, ed., (Grand Rapids, Michigan: Zondervan Publishing House, 1983), pp. 68–72.

CHAPTER EIGHT

1. Ridge Burns, "Teamwork Isn't Everything, It's the Only Thing," *Youth Worker,* Vol. II, no. IV (Winter 1986): 43–44.
2. Reginald M. McDonough, *Working With Volunteer Leaders In The Church* (Nashville, Tenn.: Broadman Press, 1976), p. 135.
3. Carol Rogers, *Learning to Feel, Feeling to Learn.*
4. Alan Loy McGinnis, *Bringing Out the Best in People* (Minneapolis, Minn.: Augsburg Publishing House, 1985), pp. 38–39
5. *Ibid.*
6. *Ibid.* p. 22.
7. *Ibid.*
8. *Ibid.* p. 131.
9. *Ibid.* p. 132.
10. *Ibid.*
11. Thomas J. Peters and Robert H. Waterman, Jr., *In Search of Excellence* (New York: Harper & Row Publishers, 1982), p. 59.
12. Alan Loy McGinnis, *The Friendship Factor* (Minneapolis, Minn.: Augsburg Publishing House, 1979), p. 100.
13. Ronald E. Wilson, "Letter From an Ex-volunteer," *Leadership,* Vol. III, no. 3 (Summer 1982): 53.
14. Stone and Miller, *Volunteer Youth Workers,* p. 68.
15. Peters and Waterman, *In Search of Excellence,* pp. 70–71.
16. McGinnis, *Bringing Out the Best,* p. 147
17. *Ibid.,* p. 148.
18. *Ibid.,* p. 159.
19. Peters and Waterman, *In Search of Excellence,* p. 223.
20. *Ibid.,* p. 69.
21. Les Christie, "There's Power In The Blood," *Youth Worker,* Vol. 1, no. 1 (Spring 1984): 107.
22. Peters and Waterman, *In Search of Excellence,* p. 202.

23. Ray Kennedy, "Howard Head says, 'I'm Giving Up the Thin World,'" *Sports Illustrated,* copyright 1980, Time Inc. ALL RIGHTS RESERVED.
24. McGinnis, *Bringing Out the Best,* p. 75.
25. *Ibid.*
26. Howard Hendricks.
27. Norris McWhirter, *1987 Guinness Book of World Records* (Sterling Publishing Co., 1986), pp. 330–331.
28. Peters and Waterman, *In Search of Excellence,* pp. 6–7.
29. Bracey and Stebe, *Identity, Intimacy, Power,* p. 89.
30. Peters and Waterman, *In Search of Excellence,* p. 236.
31. *Ibid.,* p. 80.
32. Richard Morris, "It's a Time to Do Less for Your Church Members," *Ministry: A Magazine for Clergy,* Jan. 1982, p. 4.
33. Schramm, *Gifts of Grace,* pp. 51–53.
34. McGinnis, *Bringing Out the Best,* p. 157.
35. McDonough, *Working with Volunteer Leaders,* pp. 130–131.
36. McGinnis, *Bringing Out the Best,* p. 62.
37. *Ibid.,* pp. 62–63.
38. *Ibid.,* p. 63.

CHAPTER NINE
1. Roadcup, *Methods For Youth Ministry,* p. 66.
2. Howard Hendricks.
3. McGinnis, *Bringing Out the Best in People,* p. 159.
4. Stone and Miller, *Volunteer Youth Workers,* p. 51.
5. Mark Senter, "How to Fire a Volunteer," *Group,* Vol. 12, no. 5 (May 1986): p. 66.
6. Brad Wesner, "After You've Fired Someone," *Group,* Vol. 12, no. 5 (May 1986): p. 69.

Bibliography

Ammons, Edsel Albert. *Voluntarism and the Church*. Evanston, Ill.: Bureau of Social and Religious Research, 1976.*

Anderson, James D., and Ezra Earl Jones. *The Ministry of the Laity*. New York: Harper and Row, 1985.

Bruce, A. B. *Training of the Twelve*. Grand Rapids: Kregel, 1979. First published in 1894.

Bucy, Ralph D., ed. *The New Laity*. Waco, Tex.: Word, 1978.*

Carroll, John L. *Youth Ministry: Sunday, Monday, and Every Day*. Valley Forge, Pa.: Judson, 1972.

Christie, Les. *Getting a Grip on Time Management*. Wheaton, Ill.: Victor, 1984.*

Christie, Les. *Servant Leaders in the Making*. Wheaton, Ill.: Victor, 1983.*

Concklin, Robert. *How to Get People to Do Things*. Chicago: Contemporary, 1979.

Corbett, Jan. *Creative Youth Leadership*. Valley Forge, Pa.: Judson, 1977.

Cox, Mickey, and John Denney. *Grab Bag: Resources for Youth Ministry*. Kansas City, Mo.: Beacon Hill Press.*

Crowe, Jimmy P. *Church Leader Training Handbook*. Nashville: Convention, 1974.*

Dausey, Gary. *The Youth Leader's Source Book*. Grand Rapids: Zondervan, 1983.

Driver, David E. *The Good Heart Book, A Guide to Volunteering*. Chicago: Nobel Press, 1989.

Fleischmann, Paul. *Discipling the Young Person*. San Bernardino, Calif.: Here's Life Publishers, 1985.

Foster, Richard J. *Celebration of Discipline*. San Francisco: Harper and Row, 1983.

Gangel, Kenneth O. *Leadership for Church Education*. Chicago: Moody, 1970.*

Gilbert, Sara. *Lend a Hand: The How, Where, and Why of Volunteering*. New York: Morrow Junior Books, 1988.

Greenleaf, Robert K. *Servant Leadership*. New York: Paulist Press, 1977.

Hagstrom, Richard G. *Getting Along with Yourself and Others*. Wheaton, Ill.: Tyndale, 1981.*

Haines, Michael. *Volunteers: How to Find Them, How to Keep Them.* Vancouver, B.C.: Voluntary Action Resources Center, 1977.*

Halverson, Richard, C. *A Living Fellowship: A Dynamic Witness.* Grand Rapids: Zondervan, 1977.*

Hayghe, H. V. "Volunteers in the U.S.: Who Donates the Time?" *Monthly Labor Review* 114, no. 2 (February 1991): 17.

High School Leader's Resource Volumes I and II. Wheaton, Ill.: Scripture Press, 1969.*

Holley, Robert. *Diagnosing Leader Training Needs.* Nashville: Convention, 1974.*

Hurley, Pat. *The Penetrators.* Wheaton, Ill.: SonPower/Scripture Press, 1978.*

Irving, Roy. *Youth and the Church.* Chicago: Moody Press, 1968.*

Jackson, Dave, and Neta Jackson. *Living Together in a World Falling Apart.* Carol Stream, Ill.: Creation House, 1974.*

Janowitz, Gayle. *Helping Hands.* Chicago: University of Chicago Press, 1966.

Jenkins, Jerry B. *You Can Get Through to Teens.* Wheaton, Ill.: Victor, 1972.*

Johnson, Douglas W. *The Care and Feeding of Volunteers.* Nashville: Abingdon, 1978.

Kageler, Len. *The Manual.* Camp Hill, Pa.: Christian Publications, 1983.

Kilinski, Kenneth K., and Jerry C. Woffard. *Organization and Leadership in the Local Church.* Grand Rapids: Zondervan, 1973.

King, Rosalie R., and Jacquelyn Fluke. *Volunteers: America's Hidden Resource.* Lanham, Md.: University Press of America, 1990.

Kipps, Harriet C., ed. *Volunteerism: The Directors of Organizations, Training, Programs, and Publications.* 3d ed. New York: R. W. Bowker, 1990.

Kushner, Harold S. *When All You've Ever Wanted Isn't Enough.* New York: Summit Books, 1986.

Mackenzie, Marilyn. *Dealing with Difficult Volunteers.* Downers Grove, Ill.: Heritage Arts, 1988.

McDonough, Reginald M. *Working with Volunteer Leaders in the Church.* Nashville: Broadman, 1976.

McGinnis, Alan Loy. *Bringing Out the Best in People.* Minneapolis: Augsburg, 1985.

Maslow, Abraham. *Motivation and Personality.* New York: Harper and Row, 1970.*

Menking, Stanley J. *Helping Laity Help Others.* Philadelphia: Westminster Press, 1985.

Miller, A. "The New Volunteerism." *Newsweek* (February 8, 1988), 42.

National Teacher Education Project. *Education for Volunteer Teachers.* (6947 E. MacDonald Dr., Scottsdale, AZ 85253)

Naylor, Harriet H. *Volunteers Today—Finding, Training, and Working with Them.* New York: Association, 1967.

New Roles for Youth in the School and the Community. New York: Citation, 1974.*

Newman, F. "National Policies to Encourage Service." *Change* (September/October 1989), 8.

Palmer, Bernard. *Pattern for a Total Church.* Wheaton, Ill.: Victor, 1975.*

Palmer, Parker J. *To Know As We Are Known.* San Francisco: Harper and Row, 1983.

Pearson, Darrell. *Parents as Partners in Youth Ministry.* Wheaton, Ill.: Victor, 1985.*

Pell, Arthur R. *Recruiting, Training, and Motivating Volunteer Workers.* New York: Pilot, 1977.

Peters, Thomas, and Robert Waterman, Jr. *In Search of Excellence.* New York: Harper and Row, 1982.

Qubein, Nido. *Youth Ministry Handbook.* High Point, N.C.: Nido Qubein Associates, 1975.

Releasing the Potential of the Older Volunteer. Los Angeles: Ethel Percy Andrus Gerontology Center, 1976.*

Rice, Wayne. *Junior High Ministry.* Revised Edition. Grand Rapids: Zondervan, 1987.

Richards, Lawrence O. *A Theology of Christian Education.* Grand Rapids: Zondervan, 1975.*

Richards, Lawrence O. *Youth Ministry: Its Renewal in the Local Church.* Revised Edition. Grand Rapids: Zondervan, 1986.

Richardson, Gary. *Where's It At.* Wheaton, Ill.: Victor, 1978.*

Roadcup, David. *Recruiting, Training, and Developing Volunteer Youth Workers.* Cincinnati, Ohio: Standard Publishing, 1987.

Roadcup, David. *Youth Ministry in the 80s, Volume II* (especially the chapter by Dick Alexander on "Volunteers"). Cincinnati, Ohio: Standard Publishing, 1981.

Robbins, Paul. *Leadership* 3, no. 3 (Summer 1982).

Scheitlin, George E., and Eleanor L. Gillstrom. *Recruiting and Developing Volunteer Leaders*. Philadelphia: Parish Life, 1973.*

Schindler-Rainman, Eva. *The Volunteer Community*. Washington, D.C.: Center for a Voluntary Society, 1971.*

Schramm, Mary R. *Gifts of Grace*. Minneapolis: Augsburg, 1982.

Senter, Mark. *The Art of Recruiting Volunteers*. Wheaton, Ill.: Victor, 1984.

Sexton, Floyd. "Lives of Passion and Purpose." *Modern Maturity* (August/September 1988), 82.

Sparks, Lee. *The Youth Group How-To Book*. Loveland, Colo.: Group Books, 1981.*

Stenzel, Anne K., and Helen M. Feeney. *Volunteer Training and Development*. New York: Continuum, 1976.*

Stone, David, and Rose Mary Miller. *Volunteer Youth Workers*. Loveland, Colo.: Group Books, 1985.

Stott, John R. W. *One People*. Downers Grove, Ill.: InterVarsity Press, 1968.*

Towns, Elmer L. *Successful Biblical Youth Work*. Nashville: Impact Books, 1966.*

Trueblood, David Elton. *Your Other Vocation*. New York: Harper and Row, 1952.*

Vineyard, Sue, and Steve McCurley. *Hundred and One Tips for Volunteer Recruitment*. Downers Grove, Ill.: Heritage Arts, 1988.

Wilbert, Warren N. *Teaching Christian Adults*. Grand Rapids: Baker, 1980.*

Willey, Ray, ed. *Working with Youth: A Handbook for the Eighties*. Wheaton, Ill.: Victor, 1982.*

Wilson, Marlene. *The Effective Management of Voluntary Programs*. Boulder, Colo.: Volunteer Management Association, 1976.

Wilson, Marlene. *How to Mobilize Church Volunteers*. Minneapolis: Augsburg, 1983.

Wilson, Marlene. *You Can Make a Difference: Helping Others and Yourself Through Volunteering*. Boulder, Colo.: Volunteer Management Association, 1990.

Wylie, F. W. "Crisis Time for Nonprofits." *Vital Speeches* (January 1, 1989), 170.
Youthworker 2, no. 4 (Winter 1986).
Zuck, Roy B., and Warren S. Benson. *Youth Education in the Church.* Chicago: Moody Press, 1978.

*Out of print, but still available in libraries.